LOCOMOTION PAPERS

CW01395552

The
Cirencester Branch

by
Nigel Bray

THE OAKWOOD PRESS

© Oakwood Press & Nigel Bray 1998

British Library Cataloguing in Publication Data
A Record for this book is available from the British Library
ISBN 0 85361 504 7

Typeset by Oakwood Graphics.
Repro by Ford Graphics, Ringwood, Hants.
Printed by The Pheon Press, Whitchurch, Bristol.

Hawksworth 'County' class 4-6-0 No. 1026 *County of Salop* is seen with a Cheltenham to Paddington passenger train at Kemble Junction in August 1950. The stock of the Cirencester branch train can just be seen to the right. *Real Photographs*

Front Cover: '57XX' class 0-6-0PT No. 3739 awaits departure from Cirencester station in 1956. *David Lawrence*

Title Page: Diesel railcar No. W79978 passes Chesterton Lane Halt with the 12.52 pm Kemble to Cirencester on 5th August, 1963. *M. Mensing*

Published by
The Oakwood Press
P.O. Box 13, Usk, Mon., NP5 1YS.

Contents

'57XX' class 0-6-0PT No. 3684 is ready with a passenger train for Cirencester in the branch's bay platform at Kemble. *Lens of Sutton*

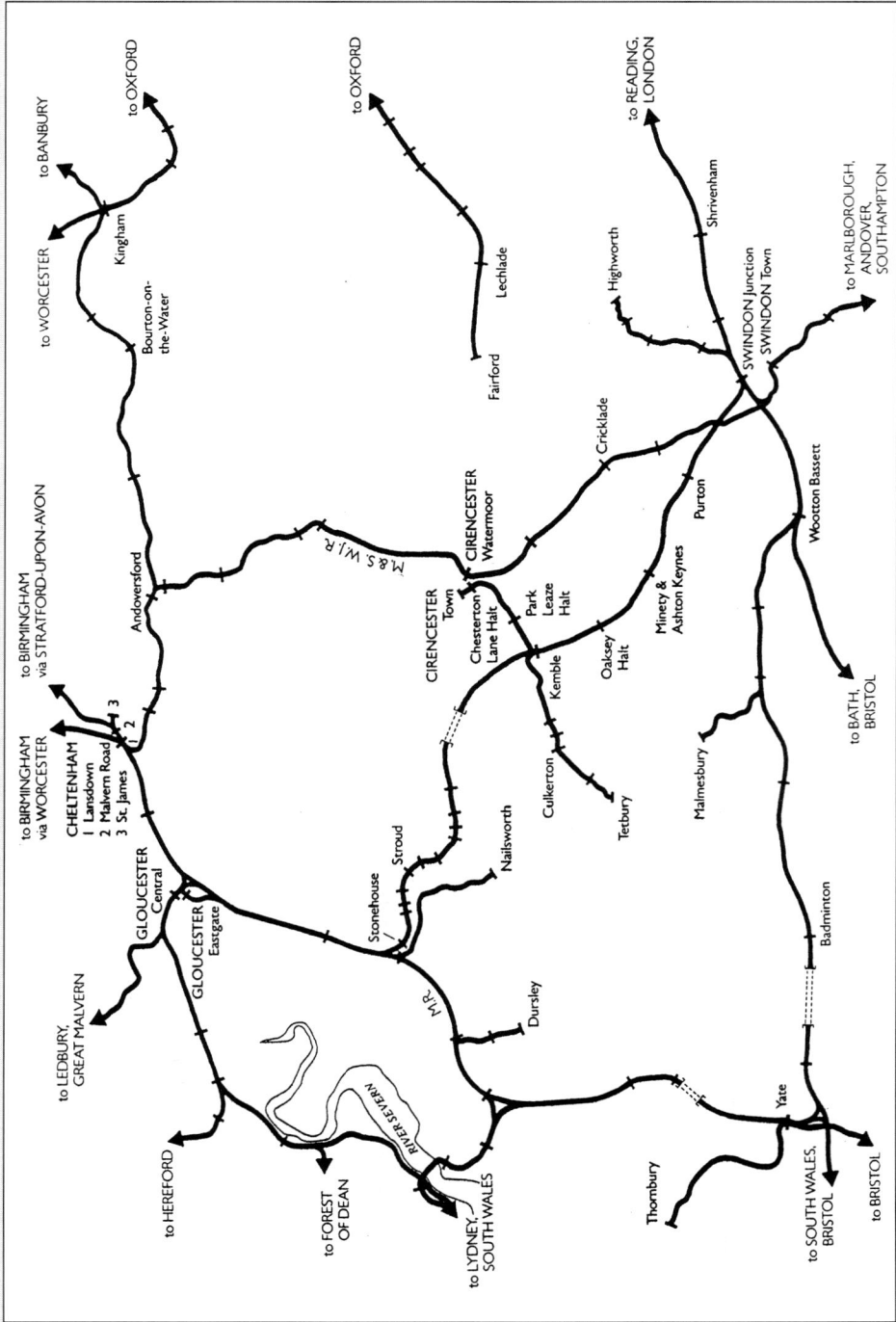

to BANBURY

to OXFORD

to WORCESTER

Kingham

Bourton-on-the-Water

to OXFORD

Lechlade

Fairford

to READING, LONDON

Shrivenham

Highworth

SWINDON Junction
SWINDON Town

to MARLBOROUGH, ANDOVER, SOUTHAMPTON

to BIRMINGHAM
via STRATFORD-UPON-AVON

Andoversford

M&SWJR

CIRENCESTER
Watermoor

Cricklade

Purton

Wootton Bassett

to BIRMINGHAM
via WORCESTER

CHELTENHAM
1 Lansdown
2 Malvern Road
3 St. James

CIRENCESTER
Town

Chesterton
Lane Halt

Park
Leaze
Halt

Kemble

Oaksey
Halt

Minety &
Ashton Keynes

to BATH, BRISTOL

GLOUCESTER
Central

GLOUCESTER
Eastgate

Stroud

Nailsworth

Culkerton

Tetbury

Malmesbury

to LEDBURY,
GREAT MALVERN

Stonehouse

M.R.

Dursley

Badminton

to HEREFORD

RIVER SEVERN

Thornbury

Yate

to FOREST
OF DEAN

to LYDNEY,
SOUTH WALES

to SOUTH WALES,
BRISTOL

to BRISTOL

Author's Note

The branch line from Kemble to Cirencester, opened in 1841 and closed in 1965, was from 1959 to 1964 the subject of an experiment in low-cost modernisation, which was overtaken by a political climate hostile to railways. It was after looking at this critical period in detail that I decided to research the history of the line.

I am particularly grateful for the expert guidance and enthusiasm of Larry Crosier of the Signalling Record Society, and John Thomas of Cirencester Railway Society. Also very helpful at crucial stages were John Nicholas, who gave me a conducted tour of present-day remains of the route; Frank Deakins, who worked at Cirencester Town in the early part of his railway career; Ian Nulty, Records Manager, Railtrack Great Western; and Mr J. Worthy of Brunel University, who assisted my research in the C.R. Clinker Collection.

Special thanks are due to Mr David Viner, Curator of the Corinium Museum, and Mr Paul Elkin, Curator of Bristol City Museum & Art Gallery, who helped me locate useful photographs. I would also like to thank Chris Leigh, Editor of *Steam World*, who is a respected authority on the railbus venture, Ross Grover, who drew the maps, and Tim Bryan, Curator of Swindon Railway Museum.

I appreciate the assistance I received from L. Beard, A.G. Biggs, B.W. Carter, C.H. Comerford, M.E. Hatch, N. Irvine, R.J.M. Keylock, K. Mulraney, D.J. Payne, D.J. Rees W.J. Roberts, P. Strong, G. Westmacott , C.F.D. Whetmath; staff at Cheltenham, Cirencester, Gloucester and Swindon public libraries; Gloucestershire County Record Office, Brunel University and the Public Record Office.

Nigel Bray
February 1998

'14XX' class 0-4-2T No. 1472 departs from Cirencester, with a special train. Railcar No. W79975, complete with white roof, is seen alongside the signal box, 5th April, 1964.

N. Potter/Corinium Museum/Cotswold District Council

Cirencester Station - Cheltenham & G.W. Union Railway

Section

Transverse Section

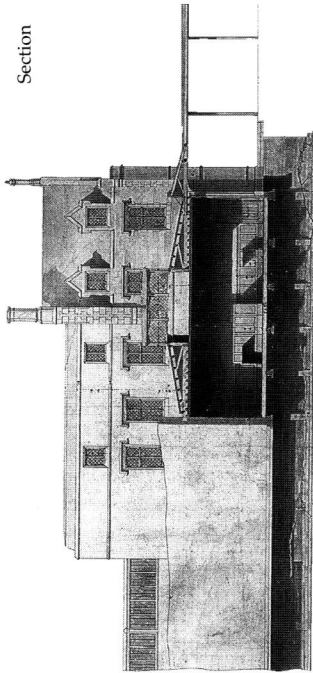

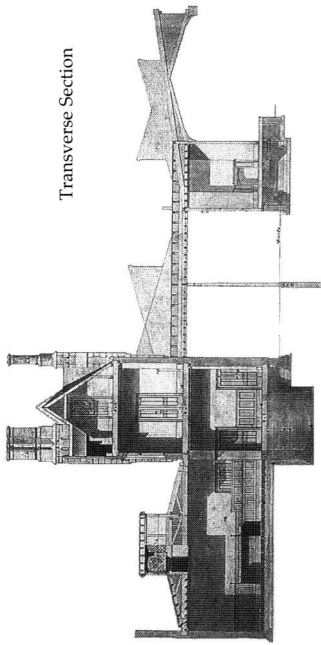

Elevation

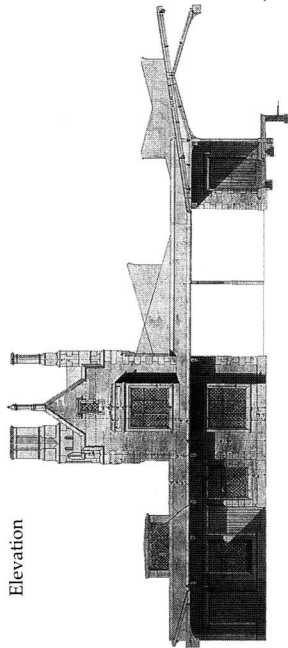

Longitudinal Section

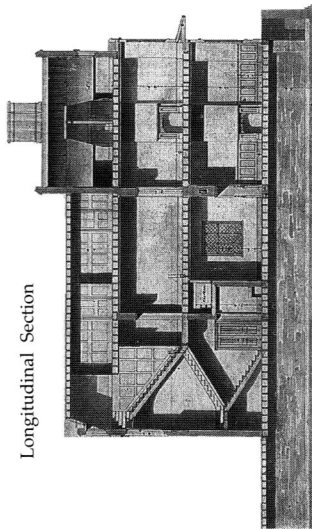

Chapter One

A Link with the Great Western

On 13th October, 1835, a few months after the Great Western Railway had received Parliamentary approval for its proposed main line from Bristol to London, a public meeting in Cheltenham unanimously resolved to promote a Bill for a railway to link up with the Great Western system by way of Gloucester and Stroud; such a line would, they claimed, produce important advantages for agriculture, manufacturing and commerce in Gloucestershire.*

The desire of Gloucestershire's leading citizens for a rail link with the capital crystallised as the Cheltenham & Great Western Union Railway (C&GWUR) Act, which received the Royal Assent only eight months later, on 21st June, 1836. The speed of progress owed much to the GWR's keen support for the scheme, which it saw as a gateway to its own entry into the Forest of Dean, South Wales and the Midlands. The C&GWUR Act provided for its broad gauge double-track line to join the Great Western 'at or near Swindon' and for a single-track branch from Kemble to Cirencester, then a town of some 5,500 people and whose markets enjoyed an extensive and long established catchment area.

The Directors of the C&GWUR, who included Cirencester Town Commissioners James Bowly, Thomas Crowther Brown and Raymond Cripps, had done a great deal of hard bargaining with opponents of the railway project in order to ensure Parliamentary approval. The strongest opposition, affecting both the proposed main line and especially the Cirencester branch, came from Robert Gordon, the Squire of Kemble House, on whose land the junction and the first seven-eighths of a mile of the branch itself were to be constructed.

Gordon had an antipathy to the new railway age and did not want his view to be disfigured (as he saw it) by this unconventional form of transport. To placate him, the company's Engineer, Isambard Kingdom Brunel, concluded an agreement on 21st March, 1836 with John Macneil, Gordon's agent. In return for £7,500 compensation and £250 expenses, Gordon agreed conditionally to release the land required for the new lines.

Among alterations Gordon stipulated to the original plans, the Cirencester branch now had to be 'carried as far north as possible' and the sides of its proposed embankment between Clayfurlong Farm and his estate boundary had to be planted with trees and shrubs to his own specification. No public station was to be erected on Gordon's land without his permission and the company would have to provide a new road bridge over the infant Thames near Clayford.† On the main line, south of where the branch would diverge, the Company was required to construct a tunnel so that the trains were not visible from Kemble House.

The 1836 Act mandated the company to maintain cuttings or embankments on the Gordon estates 'in an Ornamental Manner with good and sufficient

* Cheltenham & Great Western Union Railway Company Minutes, 19.7.1836-10.1.1843 are the source of much of this chapter.
† 6 William IV, Session 77, Clauses 15 and 16.

Cirencester Station - Cheltenham & G.W. Union Railway

Transverse Section

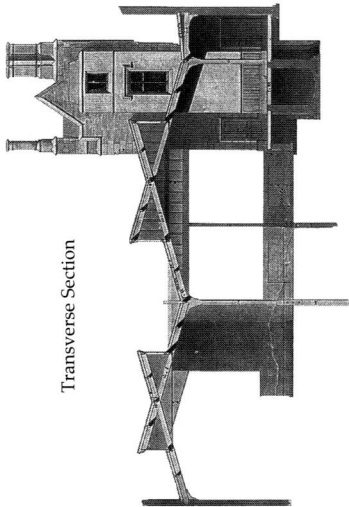

Longitudinal Section

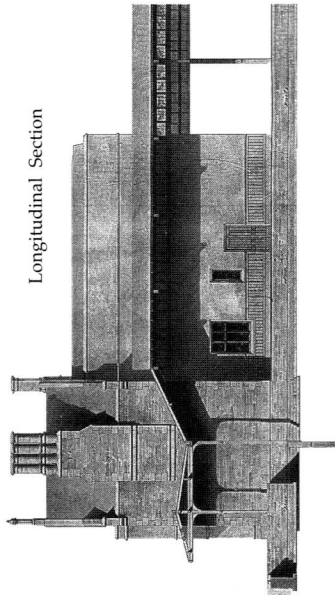

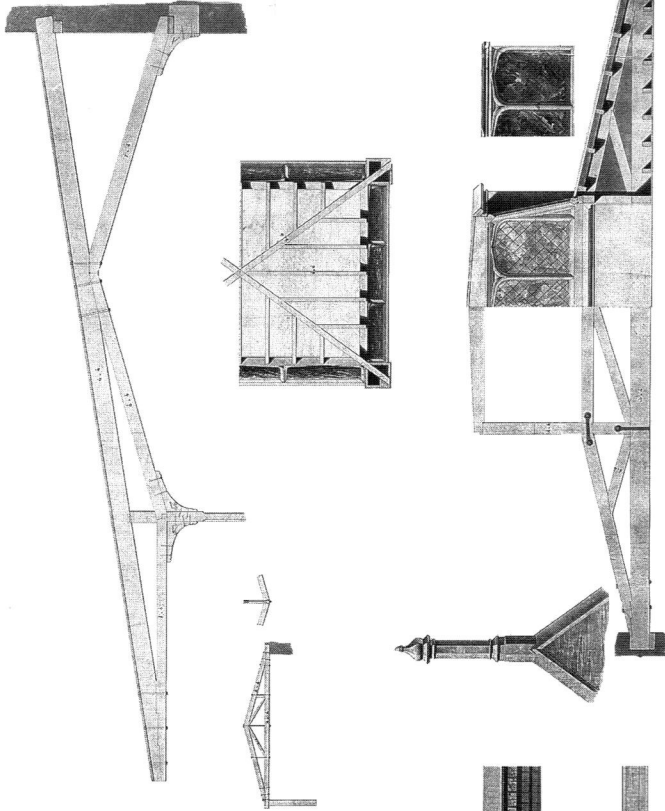

Shrubs and Forest trees' in perpetuity. The Squire, his heirs and agents were also empowered to enter these embankments or cuttings in order to improve or prune the plantations 'but so as not to impede or interfere with the proper use and maintenance of the said railway'.

This last sentence would appear to suggest that Gordon was willing, as a last resort, to prevent these cosmetic plantations from encroaching on to the running line. Or perhaps Brunel and the Directors wished to remind Gordon that, although they would do their best to accommodate his reservations about the location of the railway, he was not qualified to pontificate on the actual operation or maintenance of the lines.

Although the Act stipulated the minimum distance which the line must keep from Kemble House, it did not explicitly prohibit a public station on the estate. It merely stated that,

> No public station, yards, wharfs, waiting, loading or unloading places, warehouses or other buildings for the deposition, receiving, loading or keeping any passengers or cattle, or any . . . articles upon the estate or within 50 yards of its boundaries shall be provided without the previous consent in writing of the said Robert Gordon.*

Clearly Gordon intended to make it difficult for the C&GWUR to establish a station or sidings on his land. He probably had an eye to the possibility of additional compensation if the railway wanted to expand its activities at a later date. His agreement with the C&GWUR also secured compensation for a Mr Matthews to the tune of £250 per acre if the branch crossed a 40 acre patch of the latter's land near Ewen, about 1½ miles out of Kemble.

Finally, the promoters of the railway had to come to terms with the Thames & Severn Canal Company. In an agreement of 23rd March, 1836, the C&GWUR, promised either to donate or 'do their best to procure' land on the opposite side of the canal wharf at Cirencester to that which the company had earmarked for the station throat and loco yard

Kemble, then in Wiltshire, had been proposed in the C&GWUR Bill as the site of a triangular junction whence the Cirencester branch would leave the main line. But difficulty in raising capital for the steeply graded section of the route from Kemble to Stonehouse persuaded the Directors to open the branch simultaneously with the Kemble-Swindon stretch of the main line. By reaching an important market town as the first stage of the project, the company could expect a quicker flow of income than if it had tried to complete the main line first. Cirencester's strategic position in the road network made it a logical railhead for the transhipment of people and goods between trains, stagecoaches and carts until the main line could be completed. The turnpike road from Cheltenham to Cirencester had been completed in 1822 and would prove useful as a feeder to the developing rail network.

Incidentally, Cirencester-Swindon was not the first stage of the Cheltenham & Great Western project to open because the section from Cheltenham to Gloucester was opened, as a joint venture with the Birmingham & Gloucester Railway, on 4th November, 1840.

---

* 6 William IV, Session 77, Clause 13.

Cirencester Station - Cheltenham & G.W. Union Railway

Plan of attics

Plan view

The Directors had planned to open Swindon-Cirencester as the first stage of the project, partly because the section of main line between Kemble and Stroud involved the most expensive engineering works but also because a completed rail connection to Cirencester would bring in revenue to help finance the more difficult stages of the scheme. Perhaps the Directors foresaw the further difficulties they were to encounter with Robert Gordon in 1841 concerning release of land for the main line north of Kemble. As things turned out, Brunel had to redesign the section through Sapperton to include much steeper gradients because insufficient share capital had been raised to meet the original specification. Many shares were being forfeited by subscribers who defaulted on their payments even as the line from Swindon to Cirencester was nearing completion.

Delays in completion

Although the Cirencester branch had a gentle gradient profile, with its steepest section at 1 in 264, its opening was delayed for months by the collapse of an embankment on the main line north of Swindon. This had been formed in 1839 but by December 1840 the Directors, who had been meeting regularly at Cirencester's Ram Hotel, were feeling 'very much disappointed by the slow progress of the Works' and wanted Brunel to lean on the contractors, Elisha Oldham & Sons of Cheltenham, with a view to getting the line open by mid-January.

Brunel's reply ascribed the delay to the Swindon landslip and to 'a want of exertion' by the contractor in overcoming it. Brunel considered March 1841 to be the earliest possible opening date. The Directors then resolved to open the line on 25th March and proposed a meeting between Brunel, the company's Cirencester Committee and Messrs Oldham requiring the latter to complete all works by 15th March; this was to allow time for the statutory Board of Trade inspection.

Before the end of February, Brunel had again written to disillusion the Directors. The date of 25th March could not be met. This time they insisted on nothing less than a full explanation to their half-yearly General Meeting on 4th May. No doubt aware of his many other engineering projects, they asked him 'to disengage himself for that day' and directed him to ensure if possible the opening of the line between Cirencester and Swindon by then.

The C&GWUR needed a clear idea of when the line would open, not only to stop more shareholders from getting cold feet but also to conclude the lease of the line to the Great Western, who would operate it on behalf of the C&GWUR as provided for in the 1836 Act. The C&GWUR agreed on 15th April that the lease, to run for seven years at an annual rent of £17,000, should receive the common seal of both companies.

When the General Meeting took place, the line had still not opened but Charles Sage, the C&GWUR Chairman, explained how work had been delayed for two months by an unusually severe winter although the Directors had been confident of completion in time for the meeting, until the slip had occurred. He

Cirencester Goods Shed - Cheltenham & G.W. Union Railway

Elevation

Side Elevation

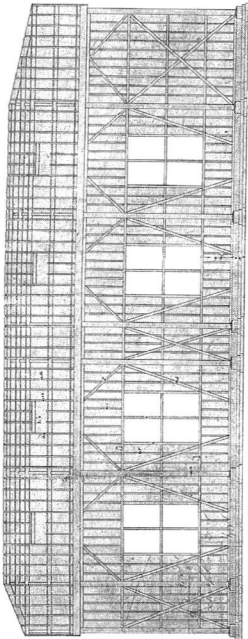

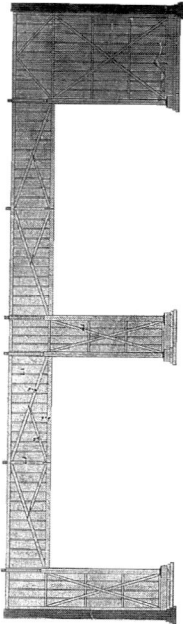

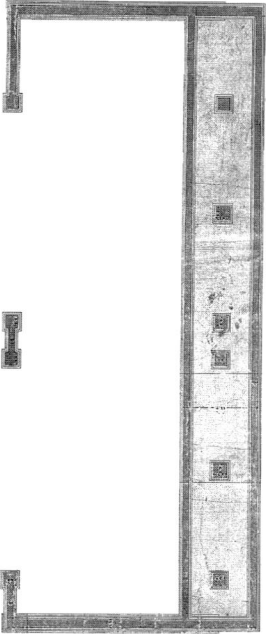

Plan of Bracing

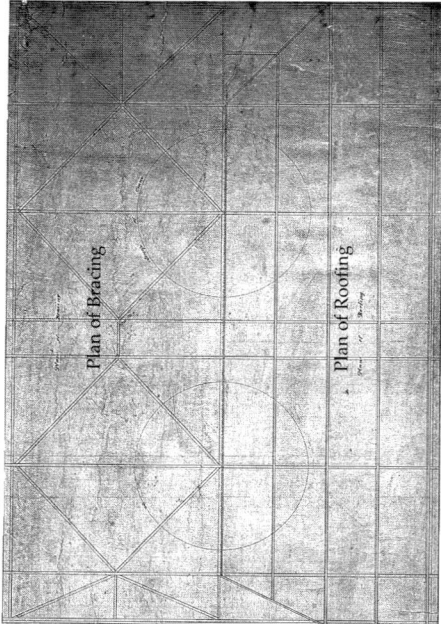

Plan of Roofing

said the Swindon embankment had been formed in good weather, except for a section built on a portion of land to which the company had been unable to get access for several months in 1839. Sage stressed that this setback had been the only misfortune suffered by the company and that the other earthworks 'stand well'.

The Chairman reported that work to date had cost the C&GWUR £352,170 16s. 4d. including Liabilities created in the Accounts for work not yet paid for. This figure represented nearly half of the authorised share capital of £750,000 for the entire project in the 1836 Act, and yet the most expensive section of the main line from Kemble to Stroud was hardly started. Sage claimed that this level of expenditure compared with other railways being built with equally heavy earthworks, and that 'nothing has been spent uselessly in the shape of decorations'.

Some of the shareholders might well have disagreed with the last remark after seeing Cirencester station building, with its highly decorative turrets and pinnacles, take shape. Brunel's design had been approved by the Directors at their meeting of 29th December, 1840 but the actual construction was supervised by his pupil Charles Richardson. More recently David Viner has suggested that Brunel had based the station architecture on his earlier design for the station at Steventon, west of Didcot on the Bristol main line, and also a substantial building in the Tudor Gothic style.*

The General Meeting at Cirencester also decided to insure two of the company's stations with the Phoenix Fire Office. Whereas the two-platformed station at Minety was to be insured for £500, the sum insured for the imposing premises at Cirencester was £4,000. The proposed lease of the line to the GWR referred to 'a principal station at Cirencester, a station for carriages . . . animals and goods at the Red Lion, Minety; and a small booking station at Purton'. Both intermediate stations were on the main line south of Kemble, none being contemplated for the Cirencester branch proper.

The dawn of Cirencester's railway age was welcomed wholeheartedly by the *Wilts & Gloucestershire Standard* despite the newspaper's professed dislike of innovations. It had, it said, always hesitated to support any apparently speculative venture before being convinced of its usefulness to the community 'but proofs the most abundant have, however, been given that the advantages that may be anticipated by the town and neighbourhood are at present incalculable'.

The editorial referred to the unprecedented changes in Swindon's economy and pace of life now that the main line from Paddington had reached there. Land prices near that line had risen, over 200 houses were being built near Swindon station and

> . . . the inhabitants, stimulated by these invigorating signs of prosperity, feel active, not dormant, members of society. So will it be with us at Cirencester; we shall enjoy a new state of existence, with the railway from Bristol to London on the one hand, and that from Gloucester to Birmingham and the North on the other.†

---

* D.J. Viner, 'Cirencester Town Station - an outline history', a report to Cirencester Development subcommittee of Cotswold District Council, November 1988.
† *Wilts & Gloucestershire Standard*, 22.5.1841.

Cirencester Goods Shed - Cheltenham & G.W. Union Railway

Transverse Section

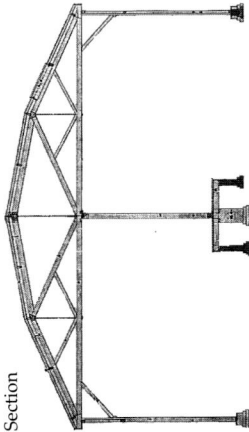

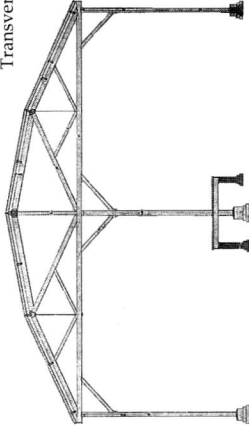

Transverse Section

Longitudinal Section

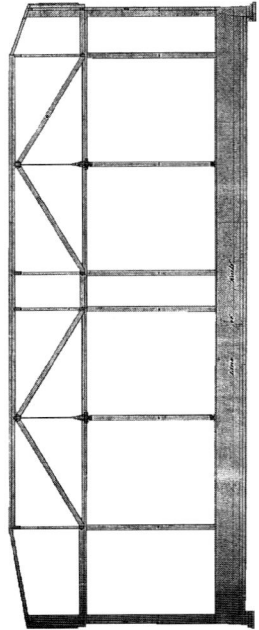

End Elevation

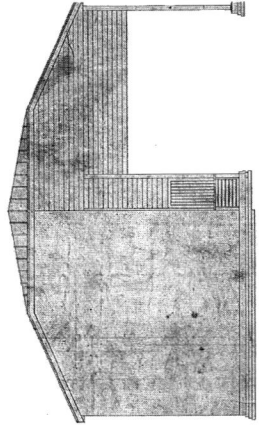

The suspense was at last lifted on 27th May, when Brunel informed the C&GWUR that the permanent way and other works would be 'in a sufficient state of advancement' to enable opening on the 31st.   Charles Saunders, Secretary of the GWR met with Thomas Crowther Brown and David Bowly to finalise operating arrangements. The lease required the GWR to construct any necessary outbuildings but as Cirencester goods shed would not be finished by opening day, the C&GWUR agreed to make an allowance to the Great Western so that it could be completed as soon as possible. At a meeting held on the 31st in the Ram Hotel, Brunel was also asked to ensure completion of the overall roof at the new terminus and also of the station fence bordering the turnpike road.

The Line opens to Cirencester

The 31st May, 1841 was also the date on which the Great Western extended its main line from Hay Lane (west of Swindon) to Chippenham and also opened Swindon station itself. But as the GWR still did not have a continuous route open between London and Bristol, the immediate effect was to make Cirencester and Chippenham joint termini of the broad gauge system from Paddington.

The first train from Cirencester to Swindon and London departed at 7.15 am after the arrival of the connecting 'Era' stage coach from Cheltenham. Commenting on 5th June that the railway enabled Cirencester people to reach London in about 3½ hours, the *Wilts & Gloucestershire Standard* reported a brisk trade at the station, 'which has all the week exhibited the stir and bustle of a fair'. Revenue from first and second class passengers had exceeded £100 per day and 'a very large traffic in goods and third class passengers had taken place'.

The earliest timetable, as summarised in GWR notices referring to the opening of services to Chippenham and 'the Cheltenham line', listed seven weekday departures from Cirencester including a mail train at 1.40 am. In the opposite direction six 'Long Trains' were shown as running from Paddington to Cirencester and Chippenham. Of these the 6.55 pm departure conveyed mail. It appears that a few additional local trains ran between Cirencester and Swindon, for the contemporary press report mentions that many of the people who caught the 7.15 am from Cirencester and detrained at Swindon were only away from home for about two hours.

Five months later the Directors reported that the line had been operating without accident or interruption, referred to economies made in working expenses and announced their recommendation of a £1 dividend payable on each £62 10s. shareholding after 24th December. This seems remarkable in view of the financial tightrope which the C&GWUR Company was now walking. For its income (principally share capital) as at 24th June had been only £300 above its aggregate Disbursements of £416,569.

For all the optimistic picture being presented by the Directors of the C&GWUR to their shareholders, there was no shortage of expense in the first years of train operation. A headache was the locomotive *Vesta*, castigated as 'breaking down when first tried and perfectly useless' even after repairs costing £470.

Cirencester Store House - Cheltenham & G.W. Union Railway

Elevation

End Elevation

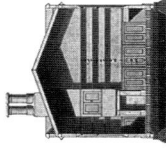

Transverse Section

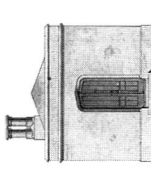

Longitudinal Section

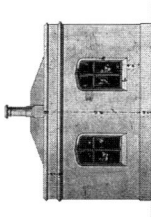

Plan

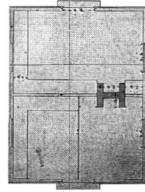

But a vastly greater call on the company's finances was the higher than expected bill from Messrs Oldham which was due for payment on 27th October, 1841. The contractors had submitted a claim for £6,714 over and above the original estimate of some £40,000 for the construction of the formation. The additional payment was claimed for unforeseen work such as repairs to the landslips on the main line at Swindon and Oaksey, and to correct inadequate measurements for side cuttings in the original survey. Around a quarter of the excess (£1,681) related to the raising of Kemble embankment on the Cirencester branch so that the underbridge at Clayfurlong Farm could clear the roadway and the Thames to comply with the 1836 Act.

Raymond Cripps and Thomas C. Brown negotiated an agreement with Messrs Oldham which fractionally reduced the latter's claim to £6,609 and provided for the revised total bill of £47,015 to be paid in three instalments. Messrs Guest & Co. also submitted their bill for £21,004 13s. 5d. which included £13,000 for rails laid between Swindon and Cirencester.

Payments arising from the finishing touches to Cirencester station were still being progressed a year or more after the line had opened. In December 1841 Stothart Slaughter & Co. of Bristol received £215 11s. 9d., for installing 'the traversing table under the passenger platform'. In the summer of 1842 the London firm of Medhurst were paid £105 for the erection of wooden drum-wheel cranes at Cirencester and Minety goods stations. Local ironmonger Henry Alexander supplied stoves and other fittings to Cirencester station at a cost of £33. The C&GWUR also had to pay him to erect iron fencing for a Mr Gregory, whose property bordered the station premises and who had received £15 11s. compensation from the railway company in 1841 for damage to his wall fruit trees. Local surveyor Thomas Lediard was paid £60 in April 1842 for making the approach roads to Querns Hill overbridge to comply with the 1836 Act. One landowner who does not seem to have been pleased with the raising of the road on the town side of this bridge was Henry Jenkins, who received £133 in damages from the C&GWUR in February 1843.

The Directors appear to have taken some trouble to find accommodation for John Ashbee, newly appointed station master at Cirencester. At first he lodged in the Watermoor area of the town but was later found a house nearer the station and on which the C&GWUR took out a seven year lease from 2nd March, 1842. The company seems to have taken up the tenancy the previous November or December because the lessor, Thomas Hall, secured payments from them of four months' rent at £35 per annum to 25 March, three months' rent at £42 per annum to 24th June and the sum of £10 to induce the previous tenant to quit.

Despite assurances to shareholders that the section of line already open was making a profit, and the promise of a 25s. dividend to be paid on each share, the C&GWUR still had a financial mountain to climb before it could open the main line through the Stroud valley. It appealed to the GWR in October 1842 either to underwrite the raising of additional capital, or to provide additional shares, to enable completion of the route from Kemble to Standish Junction by 24th June, 1845, beyond which date the C&GWUR would forfeit its half of the formation between Gloucester and Cheltenham. After a period in which the

C&GWUR Board tried to interest the GWR in taking out a 20-year lease of the company, the shareholders voted instead for absorption into the GWR with effect from 1st July, 1843. This course of action had been proposed at the C&GWUR's January General Meeting by Thomas C. Brown, who had argued that existing shareholders would enjoy greater dividends from a much larger company.

Now that the uncertainties over funding the completion of the main line had been removed, construction proceeded apace and the section from Kemble to Standish Junction opened on 12th May, 1845. Through trains began running between Gloucester and Swindon. Kemble was now a junction and the line thence to Cirencester became a 4¼ mile branch as the 1836 Act had intended. But Robert Gordon's continuing refusal of permission for a public station at Kemble meant that the Great Western was only able to provide rough wooden platforms for the interchange of passengers between the two routes. Adrian Vaughan has suggested that the exchange platforms were originally sited south of the present station. In view of what would otherwise have been a gap of almost 14 miles between Minety and Brimscombe stations on the main line, the GWR served the Kemble area by providing a station at Coates, then called Tetbury Road, where the Gloucester line crossed the Foss Way just beyond the Gordon estate.

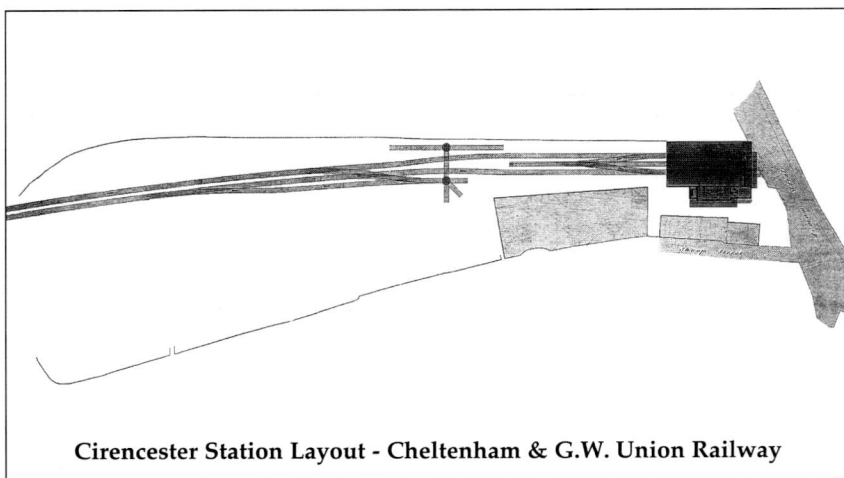

Cirencester Station Layout - Cheltenham & G.W. Union Railway

Chapter Two

A Broad Gauge Branch Line

Timetable changes from May 1845

The extension of the main line from Kemble to Standish Junction resulted in a major revision of Cirencester's train services. The junction for its connections with the rest of the Great Western system was no longer Swindon but Kemble, although no reference was made in GWR publicity or even in *Bradshaw* to the actual point of interchange. Published timetables gave a hint that Cirencester journeys might involve something out of the ordinary by including arrival and departure times for the station in both up and down tables. Another clue was to be found in the mileages which the timetables quoted from Paddington to Cirencester and Tetbury Road stations.

Cirencester gained two train departures, one at 11 am which connected into a Paddington-Cheltenham express, and a second one 20 minutes later which provided third class passengers with their 'Parliamentary' service to London, so called because the 1844 Cheap Trains Act required all railway companies to provide at least one train available to third class ticket-holders on each route. Prior to this legislation, the Great Western had been reluctant to convey the lower classes except in coal trucks at night. An edition of *Bradshaw*, issued in the earlier part of 1844, had stated that 'Third Class passengers are conveyed by the Goods Trains'. In the case of Cirencester these were 'Mixed' passenger and goods trains.

Ironically, the train service changes of May 1845 resulted in more civilised travel times for third class users of Cirencester station, not through any philanthropy on the company's part but more a side effect of Cirencester losing its night mail train. The 11.47 pm Swindon-Cirencester was withdrawn now that a connection from the 8.55 pm ex-Paddington ran through to Gloucester, serving the new Tetbury Road station. Also discontinued was the 1.40 am from Cirencester, which had conveyed mails and had also been the only morning train on which third class passengers could travel from Cirencester to London, reached at 7.45. Nor was it now necessary for someone with a third class ticket to start from Paddington at 6 or 5 am. 'Parliamentary' trains still appeared after the main timetable columns but were no longer headed as 'Passenger and Goods' or even as plain 'Goods Trains'.

There was good news for all classes of traveller in so far as fares to London were reduced, provided the main line train was not one designated as 'Express'. The single fares from Cirencester in July 1845 were 22s. 0d., first (as against 25s. 0d. in 1844); 15s. 0d. second (previously 18s. 0d.) and 7s. 11d. third (compared with 11s. 0d.). But the diversion of late night mail trains away from Cirencester, together with a later start for the first morning train (now departing Cirencester at 9.05 am) greatly reduced the scope for its inhabitants to make a day trip to the capital. The earliest arrival in Paddington was now 1.10 pm with a last train home at 5 pm, connecting to Cirencester at 8.44. This situation was much

GREAT WESTERN RAILWAY.

WESTERN DIVISION.

NOTICE IS HEREBY GIVEN, that a modification of the Railway Fares, with a view to promote an increased Passenger Traffic between CIRENCESTER and CHELTENHAM, and also between CIRENCESTER and GLOUCESTER, and other Stations, has been decided upon by the Directors, which will come into operation on the 1st of May.

The particulars may be known at the several Railway Stations.

By Order of the Directors,
THOS. GRAHAM, Superintendent.

Bristol, April 14th, 1856.

GREAT WESTERN RAILWAY.

CHEAP

EXCURSION TO LONDON

ON THE OCCASION OF THE
PEACE DEMONSTRATIONS.

On Wednesday, May 28, 1856,

AN EXCURSION TRAIN for LONDON will leave the Stroud Station at 10.50 a.m., Cirencester at 11.15 a.m., and return from Paddington at 12.0 noon, on Saturday, May 31st.

FARES FOR THE DOUBLE JOURNEY:

Closed Carriages.		First Class.
6s.	and	10s.

No Luggage beyond a Carpet Bag allowed.

N.B.—To ensure places in the Train, Tickets must be taken the previous day.

Bristol, May 14th, 1856.

GREAT WESTERN RAILWAY.

CHEAP EXCURSION TO

BATH AND BRISTOL!!!

On Thursday, June 5th,

AN EXCURSION TRAIN will start from Stroud at 7.30 a.m., calling at Brimscombe at 7.40; Cirencester at 7.50; and Swindon at 8.45 a.m.; returning from Bristol at 6.0 p.m., and Bath at 6.30 p.m. the same day.—No Luggage allowed.

FARES FOR THE DOUBLE JOURNEY:

	First Class.	Closed Carriages.
To BATH	3s. and	2s.
BRISTOL	4s. and	2s. 6d.

A GRAND FLOWER SHOW

Will be held in the Gardens of the Zoological Society at Clifton, at which the magnificent Band of Her Majesty's Royal Artillery will perform.

To insure places Tickets should be taken on the previous day.

May 14th, 1856.

Adverts from the *Wilts & Gloucestershire Standard*, 1856.

improved by the summer of 1846, when the first train departed at 7.40 am allowing an arrival in London of 11.30 for first and second class passengers but not until 2.45 pm for third class

Excursion traffic in the 1850s

Ten years after its railway had opened, Cirencester enjoyed cheap excursion fares to London, Bristol and elsewhere despite now being on a branch of the Great Western main line to Gloucester. Far from being marginalised by the steady growth of the rail network, Cirencester was brought within reach of ever more places. Completion of the South Wales Railway with the opening of Brunel's Wye Bridge at Chepstow in 1852, placed Kemble on a direct route from London to Swansea.

The Cirencester branch participated in the GWR's eagerness to exploit these new travel opportunities. Within months of the Wye Bridge being open, a special train was run from Swindon and stations in the Stroud valley (with a connection from Cirencester) to a flower show in Chepstow Castle. But the return journey went disastrously awry, taking *nine* hours to reach Swindon instead of the scheduled two and a half. The fiasco was not easily forgotten, if the letter from 'A. Grumbler, Swindon' in the *Wilts & Gloucestershire Standard* for 8th September, 1855 was anything to go by. Nor, he claimed, was such inefficiency an isolated occurrence among contemporary GWR excursions.

The highly sarcastic letter had been triggered by the Great Western's announcement of a repeat of the Chepstow trip, billed to leave Swindon at 7 am and Cirencester at 7.10 on Tuesday 11th September. Fares were 5s. 0d., first class, 3s. 0d. second class 'in closed carriages'. The band of the Coldstream Guards was to play in the castle grounds.

'Grumbler' asked whether this new trip would be 'as well organised' as the one three years earlier when an arrival home in the small hours had allowed passengers 'the advantage of sitting in the carriages nine hours without extra charge'. He then proceeded to denigrate more recent Great Western excursions, serving both Cirencester and Swindon, including one bound for Paddington on 24th August. But his most cutting remarks were reserved for a trip to Bristol which was publicised in connection with a military band at Clifton Zoo.

This heavily loaded excursion had left Cirencester at 7.50 am on Thursday 30th August. Trippers had the option of going to Bath at fares of 3s. 0d. first, 2s. 0d. second; or to Bristol for 4s. 0d. and 2s. 6d. respectively. After reversing at Swindon the train was due away at 8.45 am but, as 'Grumbler' was keen to point out, the actual departure was 9.55, behind the regular service train which the special should have preceded. Bristol was not reached until after midday but it was again the return journey which provoked his most savage humour.

Pointing out that excursionists had not been allowed to join the train at Bristol until half an hour after its scheduled departure, he commented that the delay 'allowed passengers that time to tread on each other's toes and enjoy the fragrance of each other's perspiration accompanied by the music of impatient babes in arms'. The final misfortune of the unlucky day out was a hot axlebox detected on a second class carriage near Corsham, resulting in an arrival at Cirencester after midnight. He argued that many more people would travel if the Great Western organised its special trains to run on time.*

Cheap excursions from Cirencester to London were encouraged by the Great Exhibition of 1851 and by the opening of Crystal Palace in 1854. On Saturday 1st July, less than a month after the official opening of the Palace, a special train left Cirencester at 4.45 pm, 'joining a large contribution (of passengers) from Cheltenham, Gloucester and Stroud at Kemble'. The local press reported that the trip was delayed by locomotive failure at Swindon; perhaps the Great Western considered that holders of cheap tickets (the return trip was 9s. 0d. first, 6s. 0d. second 'in closed carriages' from Cirencester) were not entitled to the most reliable motive power. The return train was due off Paddington at 6.30 pm on Monday 3rd July, the report adding that the Cirencester contingent arrived home about 10.30.†

The previous month, on Whit Tuesday, the GWR had tempted Cirencester people with a day trip to Paddington. The main train started from Cheltenham and the connection left the branch terminus at 7.50, ten minutes ahead of the first scheduled train; very possibly it was the regular train retimed. Ordinary service trains from Cirencester were sometimes billed as excursions, for example on 20th June that year when the 10.50 am connected at Kemble into a special from Paddington bound for Cheltenham, where the horticultural section of the Great Exhibition was on view. Although the return fare from Cirencester was 4s. 0d. first, 2s. 6d. second, the *Wilts & Gloucestershire Standard* considered that the higher than usual admission charge of 5s. 0d. on that day would deter many from travelling.

Neither the GWR advertisements, nor contemporary press reports, make clear whether the printed departure times of excursions from Cirencester were those of the scheduled branch trains or of special connections into a main excursion train at Kemble or Swindon. Railway companies were not eager to draw attention in print to the need to change trains even on regular services, especially in cases such as Kemble where the interchange involved traversing rough wooden platforms offering minimal comfort.

As late as July 1865 the official timetables disguised the necessity for Cirencester passengers to alight at Kemble before they could leave or join the rest of the company's system. Likewise those published in the local press in the 1870s merely quoted Cirencester arrival and departure times, listed according to which trains connected with which main line services. An added incentive to economy with the truth was that the railway did not actually serve Kemble village; its platforms were still only available for interchange purposes (and for the use of Squire Gordon's household) under the terms of the 1836 Act.

It is likely that carriages from the Cirencester branch were attached to westbound excursions at Swindon. At Kemble, however, there would have been insufficient room between the junction and the tunnel mouth for vehicles to have been easily coupled to, or detached from, a main line train.

---

* *Wilts & Gloucestershire Standard,* 1.9. and 8.9.1855.
† ibid., 24.6.1854, 8.7.1854.

Local pressure for improved services

Cirencester's Town Commissioners, while hoping the railway would attract visitors to the town, also expressed concern about the bad first impression created by the state of the road leading from the station. The *Standard* commented that 'the tourist would no longer speak of the clean town of Corinium as he walked across our streets, nearly over his shoes in mud' but also expressed confidence in the Commissioners' ability at 'getting things done . . . after a meeting or two'.*

The Town Commissioners also tried to get night mail trains restored at Cirencester, instead of the letters being taken by horse and cart to Tetbury Road station. That arrangement had been in force 10 years when, on 22nd August, 1855, a public meeting in the Town Hall called for a later collection of letters for London and expressed disquiet that the agents conveying the mailbags to Tetbury Road were 'not authorised servants of the Crown' and that security might be compromised by such arrangements. When a deputation to meet the GWR and Post Office Directors was suggested, Thomas Brewin and Robert Brown argued that postal services would be better if long-distance mails were dispatched 'by the branch trains now running instead of by the Tetbury Road carts'.†

Local representations had more success with fares. In April 1856 the Great Western began placing notices to the effect that fares would be revised from 1st May 'with a view to increasing the passenger traffic between Cirencester and Cheltenham, also between Cirencester, Gloucester and other places'. The reductions appear to have applied only to Ordinary fares, not Excursions. Two years previously the railway company had lowered first and second class single fares to London, these becoming 16s. 8d. (an impressive 25 per cent reduction) and 12s. 6d. respectively.

The minimal facilities at Kemble station still attracted criticism but it was not until the early 1880s that the Gordon family were persuaded to agree to the building of the substantial public station that is in use today. One traveller who took the inconvenience in his stride was the ventriloquist, Professor Ewart. In April 1854 he told his audience in Cirencester's Temperance Hall how he had persuaded the Kemble porter to search for an invisible passenger in a luggage van, much to the disgust of the bewildered official.#

The last years of Broad Gauge operation

In June 1865, ten trains left Cirencester on weekdays and two on Sundays. The second weekday departure, at 8.45 am, connected into an express reaching Paddington 2½ hours later. This provided the earliest arrival in London from Cirencester in that timetable, because the main line connection from the 7.55 am ex-Cirencester served practically every station, being overtaken at Didcot by the faster train. This anomaly, whereby it was advantageous to connect into the

---

* *Wilts & Gloucestershire Standard*, 6.1.1855.
† ibid., 25.8.1855.
# ibid., 29.4.1854.

second train of the day from Cheltenham to the capital, persisted for most of the life of the branch. No doubt this arrangement was to suit the lifestyle of first class travellers, who could get up later and still reach London earlier than could third class passengers, who were barred from using designated Express trains.

The 12.25 and 3.30 pm services from Cirencester also caught fast trains at Kemble which were due in Paddington at 3.0 and 6.10 pm respectively. For travellers from London, the only convenient morning train left Paddington at 9.15 am for a Cirencester arrival at 12 noon. Those willing to sacrifice a civilised hour of departure (or unable to afford first or second class fares) could travel by the 6.0 am from Paddington, changing at Swindon as well as Kemble, to reach the Cotswold capital at 10.10 am. The latest one could leave London and still reach Cirencester the same night was 4.50 pm, connecting to the branch terminus at 7.35 pm.

At this time single fares from Paddington to Cirencester were: by Express trains, 20s. 10d. first and 14s. 7d. second; by Ordinary trains, 16s. 8d. first, 12s. 6d. second and 7s. 11d. third. Cheltenham to Cirencester single fares were 4s. 6d. first, 3s. 0d. second and 2s. 3d. third.

Within five years, the branch train service had undergone some trimming. One weekday train had been withdrawn but there was now an additional trip on Sundays (5.55 pm from Cirencester, returning as 6.15 from Kemble). The weekday timetable had been slightly compressed, with the first departure from Cirencester now 8.20 am and the final evening train leaving the town at 7.05 instead of 8.00 pm. These economies were in response to the financial difficulties of the GWR and of the national economy in the late 1860s.

But freight traffic was healthy and the Great Western was later to decline requests to increase the branch passenger service at times of day when it claimed the resident locomotive was fully occupied in shunting duties.

Several main line freight services supplied or collected Cirencester wagons via Kemble. In February 1870, the 6 am goods from Swindon to Bullo Pill (a small port on the Severn estuary between Gloucester and Lydney) called at Kemble to detach wagons for Cirencester and to attach empties for Bullo off the branch. These latter wagons would have reached Kemble loaded at 3.50 pm the previous weekday via the 12.15 coal & goods ex-Bullo Pill. Loco coal wagons for Cirencester reached Kemble at 6.20 on Sunday mornings, via the 12.50 am Cardiff Newtown-Swindon Locomotive Departmental train.

The 7.05 pm departure (weekdays) from Cirencester was described as 'Passenger & Goods' in the 1870 Service Timetable, being allowed 15 minutes to reach Kemble instead of the normal ten. Two Sunday trains were also shown as 'mixed' (namely the 1.55 pm ex-Cirencester and 2.45 pm ex-Kemble) but had only 10-minute schedules. The first two weekday services from Kemble were allowed 15 minutes to reach the terminus; this suggests they were in fact 'Mixed' trains conveying wagons from early morning main line freights.

Artificial manures were a regular traffic in and out of Cirencester, being regularly promoted in the local press with the offer of free rail transport. Henry Fretwell & Co., based at Cirencester wharf, had sold blood manure since the early 1850s, 'delivered free to any station or canal wharf in London'. Companies seeking to attract business from Cotswold farmers included the

Herefordshire & South Wales Manure Company, whose agent for the Cirencester district was Mr J. Howell, of Fairford. Messrs Weedon, of Goring, Oxfordshire advertised in the Cirencester newspaper with offers of free delivery on rail for orders of at least two tons of their bone dust, bone superphosphate or Peruvian guano.

Local collection and delivery agents brought parcels, luggage and small goods consignments to and from the station. John Graham Parkinson, who had been station master at Cirencester in the 1860s, now competed with William Budd, a longer established railway agent. On 29th May, 1872, Parkinson sued his former employer in the Court of Common Pleas, complaining that his commission for rail parcel deliveries in the town was only 1s. 6d. per ton, whereas Budd received 2d. per parcel irrespective of weight.*

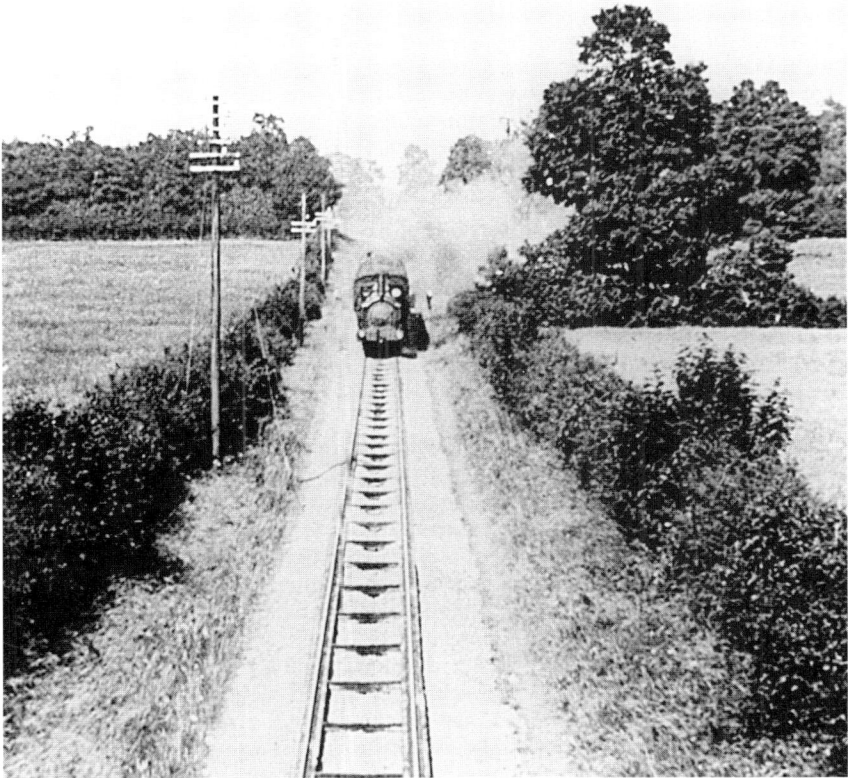

A pre-1872? broad gauge passenger train approaching Field Farm bridge, later the site of Park Leaze Halt. *Corinium Museum/Cotswold District Council*

* *Wilts & Gloucestershire Standard*, 1.6.1872.

Conversion of the Gauge

By the late 1860s the Great Western Directors were resigned to the eventual demise of the broad gauge, since the Board of Trade had recommended standardisation of the railway system on the 4 ft 8½ in. gauge adopted by all other British main line companies. In the spring of 1872 the GWR converted its South Wales main line from Swindon, through Gloucester, to Neyland (then known as New Milford), including branches.

Conversion of the Cirencester branch was scheduled to begin on Monday 20th May and to take four or five days, during which time its passengers would be conveyed by omnibus to and from Tetbury Road station instead. In the event, work did not begin until the 23rd but was still completed by the evening of Saturday the 25th, when the buses were sent back to London.* By the following Saturday, 1st June, a new service of standard gauge through trains had commenced operation between South Wales, Gloucester and Paddington.

Change of gauge resulted in a recast of the branch timetable, with two additional weekday trains from Cirencester. The earliest departure from the terminus was now 7.50 am, as against 8.20 am before the conversion, and a new service leaving Cirencester at 4.55 pm connected into a down main line train. A weakness of the final broad gauge timetable had been the lack of a connection to London between the 8.20 am and 12.10 pm trains up the branch. The new weekday service comprised 10 up and nine down trains, four of the up trains linking into Express passenger services at Kemble. But the last trip of the day was unchanged, departing Cirencester at 7.05 pm and Kemble at 7.45 pm. Sunday trains were reduced from three to two each way with the loss of the 7.10 pm Cirencester and its back working.

Kemble station rebuilding

For over 35 years Cirencester passengers had endured the very basic interchange facilities at Kemble, which afforded minimal protection from the elements. No hope of improvement was in sight until 1879, when a GWR Director was invited to stay with Earl Bathurst for the annual Vale of White Horse Hunt Ball. His experience of waiting in the draughty wooden shelter at Kemble for the branch train, in the company of some 20 other travellers, made him vow never to repeat the experience. He persuaded the GWR Board to approach Miss Anna Gordon, Robert Gordon's heir, with a view to acquiring land for a more substantial, publicly advertised station.

Miss Gordon was sufficiently amenable to the pleadings of major local landowners who supported the Great Western case that she agreed to release land for the building of a new station and branch run-round loops. This was a considerable achievement against a background of little recent capital investment by the GWR other than gauge conversion, following the collapse of its merchant bankers Overend & Gurney in 1866.

The new station buildings were opened on 1st May, 1882, coinciding with the closure of Tetbury Road station to passengers. Little expense was spared on the

* *Wilts & Gloucestershire Standard*, 1.6.1872.

buildings, constructed in sawn dressed stone with mock Tudor chimneys. The platform canopies were supported on decorative cast-iron columns and terminated in deep windowed screens. These impressive structures, largely unaltered today, were repainted as recently as March 1996.

On the up side the reconstruction was to result in an attractive walled garden in the fork of the main and branch platform faces, thanks to the enthusiasm of station master Jeremiah Greenaway.

The railway as an instrument of social mobility

The growth of the national railway network offered men from modest backgrounds an avenue of promotion that was at least equal to the opportunities in the army, navy or police force. Daniel Bingham began his celebrated career (*outlined in Appendix One*) through his appointment as a junior clerk at Cirencester, a post he owed to James Staats Forbes, who was superintendent there in the 1840s. Forbes was himself later to hold senior positions on the GWR, London, Chatham & Dover, and Dutch-Rhenish Railways. Bingham subsequently followed his patron to Paddington and the Netherlands, eventually amassing a great fortune which he was to invest to the benefit of his home town.

Harry Griffiths, appointed as booking clerk in 1870, came to be so highly regarded by the townspeople that in December 1877 fifty-three local worthies signed a letter to Sir Daniel Gooch, recommending Griffiths for promotion to station master if the vacancy should arise at Cirencester. The letter was headed by T.W. Chester Master Junior, a magistrate residing at Stratton House and who later became the town's MP; he said he had always found Griffiths 'most punctual, civil and obliging'.* But the GWR Board was unmoved, appointing Robert Murch to succeed Fred Murphy a few years later.

Appointment to station master usually involved moving away. Francis Vere Holloway, who was booking clerk at Cirencester in the early 1850s, took charge of Devizes when that station opened in 1857.

Transfer away from Cirencester did not always have a happy result. Early in 1872 William Gobey, a porter, transferred to Portskewett, Monmouthshire, 'on account of his advancing years and declining strength'. A few months later he was killed in a shunting accident at Caldicot siding. Possibly he might have been assisting with a movement that needed a younger, fitter man. Or he might have been the victim of working excessive hours, a subject which received much Parliamentary attention in the 1870s. Former workmates from Cirencester station, 'where he had been widely known and much respected' during the 22 years he had been based there, carried his coffin to the Noncomformist burial ground in Watermoor Road.†

The branch train acted as ambulance in May 1882 after Daniel Biggs, a railway labourer, was injured while repairing a bridge on the main line near Minety. The brickwork and scaffolding gave way and he was buried under the debris, breaking a thigh. He was 'extricated with care' and conveyed by train to Cirencester, where he was detained at the Cottage Hospital, which Earl Bathurst had founded in 1875.#

* PRO Ref. RAIL 256/86.
† *Wilts & Gloucestershire Standard*, 8 6., 15.6.1872.
# *Wilts & Gloucestershire Standard*, 27. 5.1882.

Chapter Three

The Great Western is Challenged

Despite the decline of its textile industries in early- and mid-Victorian times, Cirencester consolidated its position as capital of East Gloucestershire as the century progressed. The Corn Hall which opened in 1862 and the cattle market in 1867 were signs of a growing local economy which provided more business for the branch line to Kemble. But many of the town's leading citizens considered it got a raw deal from the GWR as far as freight rates and passenger train services were concerned. This discontent crystallised, not only into calls for existing facilities to be improved, but also into active support for the Great Western's potential local competitors. The Town Commissioners pinned their hopes on a revival of the Cirencester arm of the Thames & Severn Canal but the Local Board of Health, which replaced the Town Commission under a reorganisation of Local Government in 1876, preferred to back rival local railway schemes.

A victory in the campaign to enhance the existing line had been the GWR's agreement in October 1874 to provide better facilities for handling livestock at Cirencester. Robert Anderson had drawn his fellow Commissioners' attention to the unsatisfactory arrangements the railway had for the transhipment of animals sold in the new livestock market. On 29th May John Burgess had won a motion condemning the situation whereby animals sold in the market were driven along Tetbury Road past the station forecourt and then through Sheep Street to the goods yard; this, he claimed, obstructed the highway, was very time-consuming and cruel to the beasts.

The Commissioners knew that Earl Bathurst, who had funded the new cattle market, also owned land immediately west of the station and had offered to provide facilities by which animals could be conveyed to and from trains without having to use public streets. Accordingly, they urged the railway company to construct a new cattle dock. Further impetus came from Cirencester Chamber of Agriculture's request for a meeting with Great Western officials to discuss the issue. So the Commission empowered its Chairman, foundry owner Henry Alexander, to represent it in any combined delegation, which would also complain about the 'inadequate' goods yard crane, a great obstruction to trade. Alexander obtained an interview with James Grierson, the GWR General Manager, following it up with a letter seeking confirmation of the company's intentions. Grierson replied that the necessary capital works 'should be completed forthwith'.* Earl Bathurst's support had been the catalyst but Grierson deserves much of the credit. He was an energetic manager who acted upon many constructive suggestions from local authorities elsewhere in the company's territory.

But it was the threat of competition which did most to induce the Great Western to make concessions to its customers in Cirencester. In 1881 the Local Board of Health supported petitions in favour of the proposed Swindon &

---

* Cirencester Town Commissioners, Book of Proceedings.

Cheltenham Extension Railway (S&CER) which would put the town on a north-south route connecting the Swindon, Marlborough & Andover Railway (SM&A) (then under construction) with the Midland Railway (MR) at Cheltenham. Had the S&CER's longer term plans materialised, Cirencester would have become a crossroads of Cotswold lines. For the 1881 Bill also sought powers for a link from Cirencester to Fairford, already the terminus of a branch from Oxford. And the S&CER was canvassing support for another east-west line from Siddington, south of Cirencester, to reach the Midland at Nailsworth by way of Kemble (where it would pass under the GW main line) and Tetbury.

The Swindon & Cheltenham Directors felt they could exploit Cirencester's dissatisfaction with the GWR in order to win capital for their own projects. A meeting was held in February 1883 at the White Hart Assembly Rooms, Tetbury to promote the Siddington Nailsworth scheme. Several speakers from the floor were members of Cirencester Local Board at pains to point out the iniquities of the Great Western's local monopoly. William Cripps blamed the high price of coal, which then sold at 21s. 0d. per ton in Cirencester, on recent increases in GWR freight rates.* W.H. Cole, of Cole & Lewis' bacon factory, told the meeting how he had persuaded the Great Western to offer a competitive rate for the transport of sheep from Bristol to Cirencester.

Cole said that for years he had been paying 42s. 0d., per truck of 30 sheep from Bristol via Swindon. But he had discovered he could save 18s. 0d. on each truckload by using the Midland line from Bristol to Stonehouse, thence by Great Western from Stonehouse to Cirencester. After he had drawn this anomaly to the GWR's attention, the company had (eventually) agreed to offer a rate of 24s. 0d. per truckload over its own route via Swindon. Not only was he now paying less but he had saved the bother of having to get his animals unloaded and retrucked at Stonehouse. He claimed that thousands of Cotswold sheep had been conveyed to Bristol and Bath since he had driven this bargain with the GWR.

Cirencester now enjoyed more favourable rates for conveying not only sheep but corn, cattle cake and manures to and from Bristol over the Great Western system. These charges now undercut its rates for carrying the same cargoes between Bristol and Purton which was a shorter journey by 12 miles.

Cole also highlighted the Great Western's very favourable rate for transporting sheep between Bristol and Stroud (at 14s. 6d. per truckload) despite traversing a greater mileage over the company's metals than to Cirencester. This was to compete with the Midland whose Stroud branch terminus was yards from the Great Western station. But he cited Stonehouse, which the MR served directly from Bristol, as enjoying the best deal of all. For although the Great Western's standard tariff per ton of corn, cake or manure between Stonehouse and Bristol was 4s. 2d. (as against 5s. 0d. for Bristol/Stroud and 5s. 10d. for Bristol/Cirencester), it was now prepared to offer a special rate for four-ton lots at 3s. 4d. per ton. Advancing these prices as a case for more competition, he claimed that the GWR had been more attentive to its customers at Cirencester since the rival S&CER line had been proposed.

* *Wilts & Gloucestershire Standard*, 3.3.1883.

Clearly Cirencester businessmen hoped that additional railways putting the town strategically on long distance routes, as distinct from being just the terminus of a short branch, would not only provide faster access to distant markets but put them in a much stronger bargaining position with railway companies. For Cole had demonstrated that, whatever people might say about the Great Western, it had been willing to lower its freight charges rather than see its business defect to a rival whose route was shorter.

Matters progressed rapidly in 1884 after the town celebrated the arrival of its long awaited competing railway. The S&CER had opened from Rushey Platt, on the SM&A north of Swindon, to its own Cirencester station, about half a mile east of the GWR terminus, on 1st November, 1883 for goods and 8th January, 1884 for passengers. A Bill to amalgamate the S&CER and SM&A companies as the Midland & South Western Junction Railway (M&SWJ) received the Royal Assent on 23rd June. Included in the Bill had been revised proposals for a triangular junction at Siddington, whence a new line would veer north-westerly to join the GW Cirencester branch, in a junction facing Kemble, near Siddington Field Farm. Another chord was proposed from the GW branch near Ewen, avoiding Kemble and following the route of the canal to join the Swindon-Gloucester line near Thames Head. Together with the S&CE's earlier Cirencester-Fairford scheme, the new plans represented a scaled-down version of the grandiose plan for an east-west route connecting Oxford, Cirencester and South Wales.

The most significant difference between the M&SWJR's 1884 Act and the earlier S&CER proposal was that the new company no longer had designs on Tetbury. For the Great Western had cleverly deposited a Bill for a Kemble-Tetbury branch in November 1883; this received the Royal Assent on 7th August 1884 and the line opened on 2nd December, 1889.

The Great Western could claim by the late 1880s to have emerged triumphant from what had seemed at times a major threat to its domination of the Cotswolds. It had effectively closed the Thames & Severn Canal which had still carried a limited traffic in roadstone and building materials until 1887. The GWR's modest Tetbury branch and the serious financial difficulties which beset the M&SWJ for most of the decade had thwarted the latter company's hopes of expansion westward. What is more the Great Western would still enjoy running powers eastwards if the Siddington triangle and Fairford extension ever became a reality. These two links would have upgraded the Cirencester-Kemble branch but might eventually have undermined the GWR station in Cirencester. For the junction at Siddington empowered by the 1884 Act would have enabled GW trains to run into the M&SWJ station at Cirencester but not vice versa. The terminus station might then have become the target for economies after the Great Western absorbed the M&SWJ in the 1923 Grouping; as was to happen in 1933 at Marlborough where the original GW station closed to passengers and its services were diverted into the M&SWJ through station.

The complaints continue

The Midland & South Western's weak finances and the engineering problems it encountered north of Cirencester prevented its trains from reaching Cheltenham until 30th June 1891. But even after this Cirencester Local Board was regularly pursuing complaints with the GWR about the deficiencies of its services to the town. Ironically this could be regarded as a compliment to the Great Western in that its branch to Kemble, notwithstanding the arrival of a competitor, was still regarded locally as the town's main gateway to London and the West of England.

Leading citizens tried for years to get more frequent passenger services over the branch. It was not only gaps in the service between Cirencester and Kemble but also between Swindon and Gloucester which aroused complaints. Cirencester Local Board joined forces with Stroud Chamber of Commerce in spring 1891 to press for reinstatement of a Swindon-Cheltenham train which used to provide a connection from the 9.00 am ex-Paddington. There was currently no connection to Cirencester between the 5.30 am and 10.20 am departures from Paddington. The Local Board put forward the reasonable enough argument that a mid-morning service from the capital would enable London businessmen to do a day's business in Gloucestershire and still return the same day.

The previous autumn the Local Board had pressed the GWR to provide a Cirencester connection out of the 5.50 pm Gloucester-Swindon, due Kemble at 6.34. As things then stood, the next available branch train did not reach Cirencester until 8.10 pm, a fate sometimes suffered by passengers using the 3.41 pm ex-Bristol which had a tight connection at Swindon.*

But the Great Western was unimpressed, claiming that the branch engine was fully occupied in shunting during the times suggested for additional trains, and that the cost of steaming a second engine would much outweigh any likely extra revenue. These arguments did not convince the Local Board. William Cripps recalled a similar reply some years earlier to the effect that the branch could not have a passenger train between 9 am and 1 pm because of shunting commitments at Cirencester. He described the company's attitude as ridiculous because a passenger train took only seven minutes each way to traverse the branch.†

It is hardly surprising, given the GWR's resistance to these calls to improve its passenger service to the town, that the Local Board (and its successor from 1895, the Urban District Council) supported attempts to take the canal out of GWR control and into a public Trust managed by Allied Navigations and local authorities. Robert Anderson, the UDC's first Chairman and also agent for Earl Bathurst, reacted to a 5 per cent increase in railway freight rates by saying that the only way to persuade companies to keep their charges reasonable lay in healthy, vigorous competition. If properly maintained and managed, the canal offered 'the only effective competitive force'.#

---

* Cirencester Local Board Minutes.
† *Wilts & Gloucestershire Standard*, 1.10.1890.
# Cirencester UDC Minutes, 23.2.1895.

A view of Cirencester station building and horse dock, showing the canopy over the west loading bay and screen around the platform buffer stops. The overall roof has been removed (i.e. post-1874) but sleepers are similar to broad gauge tie bars.

Roger Carpenter Collection

The councillors cannot have had any illusions about the canal's ability to compete with rail transport. Early in 1898 they learned from the newly formed Thames & Severn Canal Trust that no boats could travel from Daneway, west of Sapperton canal tunnel, to Cirencester or Lechlade until leaks had been stopped in the summit of the waterway. The Council was in any case a very good customer of the GWR for transporting building materials required for its ambitious schemes to improve the town's sewers and widen Castle Street, which its Streets Committee described as 'an important link between the town centre and the GWR station'.

Regular consignments arriving in the second half of the 1890s included granite in blocks, broken stones and chippings from the Clee Hill Granite Company, Shropshire; guttering and stone blocks from the Mendip Granite & Asphalt Company of Cranmore, Somerset; cement from Bristol and service pipes from the Albion Clay Company. Free rail transport appears to have been offered as an incentive to buy in bulk from suppliers who had their own wagons and who were able to recoup the GWR's freight charges by winning big orders. For example, in June 1896 the UDC ordered 400 tons of handbroken Clee Hill stone at 11s. 11d. per ton and 200 tons of Clee Hill chippings at 9s. 6d. per ton, delivered free to the GWR station.

As well as playing a key role in this public works programme, the branch line witnessed another aspect of local pride on 25th July, 1895 when it conveyed the Prince of Wales on his visit to the Royal Agricultural College, celebrating its 50th anniversary, and to the Gloucestershire County Agricultural Show, also in Cirencester. The UDC banned horses, carriages and carts from Tetbury Road between the station forecourt and the Avenue entrance to the college from 1 till 2 pm.

View of Kemble Junction from the Swindon end c. 1900.   *Lens of Sutton*

A superb view of Cirencester goods shed c. 1900, looking towards the station.

British Railways/Corinium Museum/Cotswold District Council

Chapter Four

Expansion Frustrated

The Cirencester-Fairford Light Railway scheme

With two railways now firmly established at Cirencester, there were renewed calls for the local network to be expanded by joining up separate routes. The proposal made in 1906 was for a light railway linking the town with Fairford, the terminus of the East Gloucestershire Railway branch from Oxford which the GWR had absorbed in 1890. The new route would have created the triangular Junctions at Siddington which had featured in the 1883 scheme for a link between the M&SWJ and South Wales.

Had it materialised, the 9½ mile line would not only have produced a direct route between Cirencester and Oxford but would also have brought longer-distance trains on to the Kemble-Cirencester branch. It would have shortened the Cirencester-Paddington distance by six miles, although it is very doubtful that this would have resulted in a faster journey to London because the route would have involved some 30 miles travelling over single track to reach main line trains at Oxford.

In an effort to attract capital, the promoters prepared a Prospectus which painted a favourable picture of the anticipated revenue and operating costs. New stations were proposed at Siddington, Preston, Ampney, Maisey Hampton, Poulton, Harnhill and Fairford West.

The scheme did not enjoy the support of the two existing companies serving Cirencester. The Prospectus admitted that the M&SWJ opposed the project; ironically much of the financial case for the new line was presented by J.F.R. Daniel, a former General Manager of the Midland & South Western Junction. He also conceded that the Great Western had declined to work the new line but was confident that they would eventually do so.

His optimism was based on estimated annual working expenses of £3,663 and revenue of £7,904. Nevertheless, the promoters required capital of £90,000 to start the project, including £66,517 for actual construction. But on their own admission, a dividend would not be payable until 40 years after services began running!*

In the event, the scheme was sunk by the refusal of Gloucestershire County Council to pay a capital grant. The Great Western was at this time too heavily involved with building its own new main lines such as Cheltenham-Honeybourne and the Castle Cary-Langport route, seriously to consider diverting funds to create a new branch line which was not expected to be profitable in the foreseeable future.

---

* Correspondence and pamphlets in Gloucester Reference Library, refs. 14.25, 14.76, 14.77.

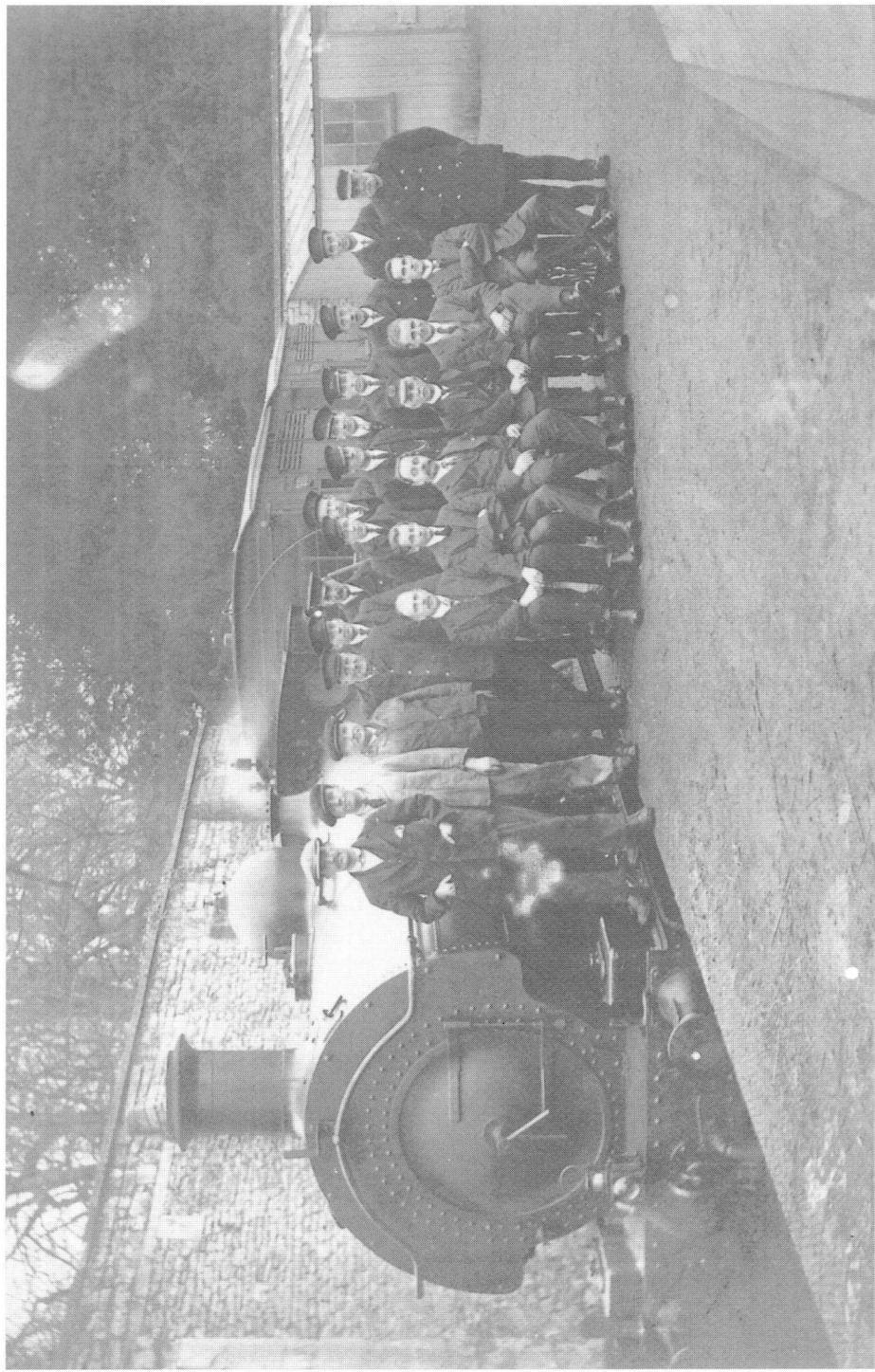

Cirencester station staff are seen in a posed group beside an unidentified saddle tank with two horseboxes at the buffer stops c. 1900.

Train services on the Branch

Ironically the early years of the century saw a boom in rail traffic. The Cirencester-Kemble passenger service expanded to 14 trains each way on weekdays in 1902, when one down and two up trains were 'Mixed'. The fastest journey from London to Cirencester at this time was provided by the 'Cheltenham Spa Express', 3.15 pm from Paddington, which connected into the 5.17 from Kemble arriving Cirencester at 5.30 pm.

By 1906 a Railmotor train was operating a direct round trip between Swindon and Cirencester on Monday afternoons. Railmotors had first been introduced on the GWR in 1903 and consisted of a locomotive enclosed in a third class carriage. Railmotors could be driven from either end of the vehicle, dispensing with the need to run the engine round its train at the end of a journey and thus allowing more frequent or longer-distance services to be run.

In July 1906 the Monday Railmotor was due in Cirencester at 2.50 pm, returning for Swindon five minutes later. It was a useful train home for shoppers living in Minety and Furton who otherwise had to change at Kemble, and for farmers who had been to Cirencester's monthly cattle market.

It appears that this Railmotor trip was made possible by a spare Diagram which had been devised to cover for any failures in the intensive Railmotor services then operating in the Stroud Valley. The Service Timetable for summer 1906 shows the train headed up as 'Passenger or Motor'; five years later, Rail Motor Car Diagram No. 10 shows only the one working from Swindon and back.

An interesting working in the same (1906) timetable was the 4.10 pm 'Mixed' train from Cirencester, conveying four Station Trucks which were attached to long-distance freight trains at Kemble. Station Trucks carried railway stores and small consignments of freight. Two years later, these four vehicles serving Cirencester were working to and from Birkenhead, Birmingham (Hockley), Cardiff and Manchester.*

The Railmotor service appears to have continued up to the outbreak of the Great War. *Bradshaw* for August 1914 showed the Mondays-only Swindon through train in a branch service amounting to 12 down trains on Mondays and Saturdays, 11 down trains on other weekdays; in the up direction there were 13 trains on Mondays, compared with 12 on other weekdays. Sunday trains were two each way, one early afternoon and the other early evening.

---

* A. Vaughan, *GWR Junction Stations*. There is also an instruction in the Sectional Appendix to the 1914 Service Timetable, Area No. 7, relating to the working of Cirencester Station Trucks at Kemble, as follows:

> The Cirencester Station Truck will stand on the branch platform line every night after the last train has left for Cirencester, for the purpose of transhipping the Station Truck goods. The truck shall be placed in a siding by the engine of the first train arriving at the station after the truck has been unloaded. In no case, however, must a truck be so placed when a train is due for Cirencester. A lamp showing a red light must be placed at the end of the truck so as to be seen by the (Kemble East) Signalman during the time it is at the platform line.

> The Signalman must always be told by the Night Porter when a truck has been placed on the Platform Line and when it has been removed.

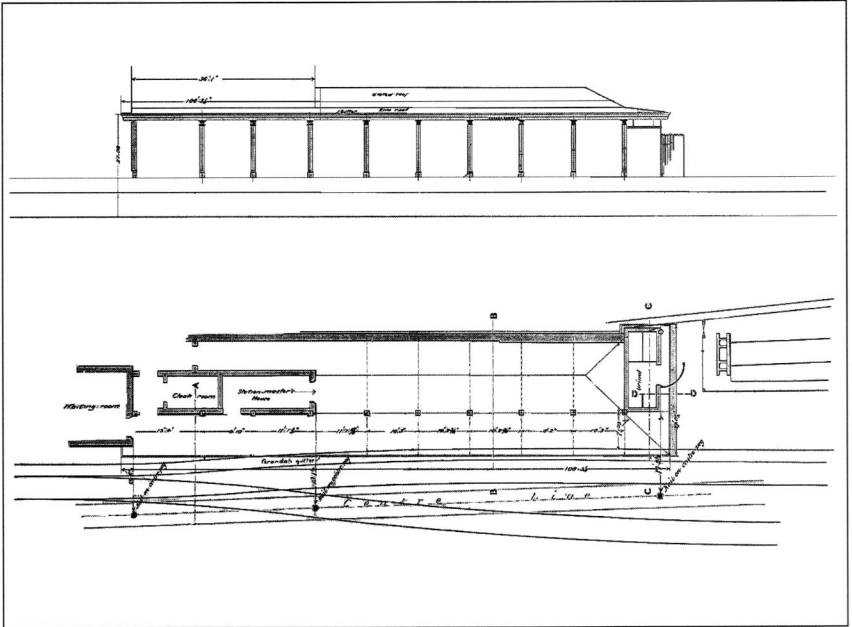

Plan view and elevation of Cirencester station platform canopy as surveyed in June 1913.

Excursion traffic increased during the 10 years prior to the war and the Great Western became more bullish in placing prominent adverts in the *Wilts & Gloucestershire Standard*. These included trips to London in the winter months, aimed at pantomimes and shopping.

When it came to seeking business from Cirencester people planning to visit Cheltenham Races, the Great Western had an advantage over its rival, the M&SWJ, despite the handicap of a much longer and less direct route. The Cheltenham-Honeybourne line, opened in 1908 to create the GWR's own route between Gloucester and Birmingham, included a station right beside the racecourse. Excursionists in March 1913 could leave Cirencester at 9.27 am to reach the Racecourse station at 11 o'clock.

Racegoers to Newbury were offered a journey of a little over two hours from Cirencester, departing at 10.10 am and changing at Kemble. The homeward train left Newbury around 5 pm. One- or two-day tickets were available for those travelling out on Friday 14th March, 1913, and a half-day ticket using a later train was aimed at people who worked on Saturday mornings.

For those able to afford the time and expense, eight or 11-day excursions to Ireland were available, via Fishguard Harbour which had become the company's main Irish port in 1906. Also promoted as Easter breaks from Cirencester at this time were tickets involving outward travel on the Thursday to popular resorts in the West Country and North Wales, and on the South and East Coasts.

On Easter Monday 1913, Cheap Day Return fares were on sale to a great variety of destinations within about 40-50 miles of Cirencester, including Chepstow, Hereford, Malvern, Stratford-upon-Avon and Warwick. The two last-mentioned had become feasible day trip destinations with the opening of the Cheltenham-Honeybourne line in 1908. Less easy to reach, despite the inducement of cheap fares, were Symonds Yat and Coleford (both normally involving two further changes after Kemble); such protracted journeys may have delighted the enthusiast but had much less appeal to the average passenger.

World War I

The war did not drastically affect the level of train services at first. Cheap excursion tickets remained available until the drastic nationwide service cuts of 1917, although publicity was greatly scaled down. For instance, in the early months of 1915 the *Wilts & Gloucestershire Standard* reproduced small notices mentioning in general terms the availability of cheap GWR excursions to London. A more specific notice referred to cheap tickets for one, two, four or six days, travelling out by the 8.10 am from Cirencester on Wednesday 10th February.

No reference to excursions, or even to times of scheduled trains has been found in issues of the *Standard* for 1916. Perhaps a growing awareness of the realities of war, including the introduction of conscription that year and a regular traffic in visitors to wounded servicemen in London hospitals, made it inappropriate for railway companies to publicise pleasure trips, quite apart from the problems of depleted manpower and the mounting pressures to use locomotive and rolling stock to run supply and troop trains.

By December 1915 the branch passenger timetable had been reduced to 10 round trips on weekdays. The two Sunday trains each way remained and indeed survived a further round of economies which were to cut the weekday departures from Cirencester to eight daily by August 1917. Good connections at Kemble still enabled someone leaving Cirencester on a Sunday afternoon to reach Paddington that evening, or alternatively to spend 2½ hours in Gloucester before returning via the evening train down the branch.

By the end of 1917 one-third of the GWR workforce had been called up. Leisure travel was discouraged by a 50 per cent fares rise that year. Not surprisingly, there was another round of cuts in passenger trains throughout the system. The April 1918 timetable for the Cirencester branch amounted to just six journeys each way, weekdays only. What is remarkable, in this weakest ever service in the line's history, is that the schedules spanned the same 12½ hour period as they had done pre-war, with a first train from Cirencester at 7.50 am and the final departure from Kemble at 8.22 pm. It therefore remained possible to reach Paddington at 10.45 am and return on the 6 pm service the same day, using the branch trains.

Less surprising was the withdrawal of Sunday trains from the branch, these not being restored until 1928. By contrast, the M&SWJ continued to run a limited Sunday service, probably because their line was of greater strategic importance in the war effort, providing a north-south route for troop trains and serving a number of army camps directly.

KEMBLE AND CIRENCESTER BRANCH.

SINGLE LINE.—Worked by Electric Train Staff and Block Telegraph.

WEEK DAYS.

Distance.		Station No.	1	2	3	4	5	6	7	8	9	10	11
				Mixed		Pass.	Pass.			Mixed ST 20		Swindon Pass.	
M. C.				A.M.		A.M.	A.M.			P.M.		P.M.	
	Kemble dep.	2503		8 40	..	9 45	10 30	..	..	1 20	..	2 27	..
4 16	Cirencester arr.	2509		8 50	....	9 53	10 38	....	....	1 30	....	2X35	....

WEEK DAYS.

		12	13	14	15	16	17	18	19	20	21
			Pass. ST 7 11		Pass.		Pass.	Light Engine.	Pass.		Goods
			P.M.		P.M.		P.M.	P.M.	P.M.		P.M.
Kemble dep.		..	3 45	..	5 20	..	6 37	7 30	8 25	..	9 15	..	..	..
Cirencester arr.		....	3 53	....	5 28	....	6 45	7 38	8 33	....	9 28	....	....	..

WEEK DAYS.

		1	2	3	4	5	6	7	8	9	10	11	12
			Pass.		Pass.		Pass.		Pass.		Goods.		Swindon Pass.
			A.M.		A.M.		A.M.		P.M.		P.M		P.M.
Cirencester.... dep.			7 50	..	9 30	..	10 0	..	12 30	..	2X37	..	3 0
Kemble .. arr.			7 58	...	9 38	...	10 8	....	12 38	....	2 47	....	3 8

WEEK DAYS.

		13	14	15	16	17	18	19	20	21
			Mixed Q		Pass.		Goods	Mixed		Light Engine
			P.M.		P.M.		P.M.	P.M.		P.M.
Cirencester .... dep.		..	4 40	..	6 10	..	7 0	7 45	..	8 35	..	..	..
Kemble .. .. arr.		....	4 50	....	6 18	....	7 10	7 55	....	8 43	....	....	....

Q May convey 10 wagons of Down Line Traffic and S.T. traffic.
Side lamps not carried on Passenger trains on this Branch.

KEMBLE AND TETBURY BRANCH.

Worked by Electric Train Staff and Block Telegraph between Kemble and Tetbury without any intermediate Signal Station. **Culkerton Station.**—The Sidings at Culkerton are locked by a key fixed in end of the Electric Train Staff.

Distance.	**DOWN TRAINS.** WEEK DAYS.	Station No.	1	2	3	4	5	6	7	8	SUNDAYS.
			Mixed	Mixed		Pass.		Pass.		ass.	Pass.
M. C.			A.M.	A.M.		P.M.		P.M.		P.M.	P M.
	Kemble.... ... dep.	2503	8 45	10 50	....	1 28	....	5 20	....	6 55	8 15
3 3	Rodmarton Platfm ,,	2505	8 53	10 57	..	1 35	..	5 27	..	7 2	...	8 23
4 31	Culkerton .. { arr.		8 59	11 1	....	1 39	....	5 31	....	7 6	...	8 27
	Culkerton .. { dep.	2506	9 0	11 10	..	1 40	..	5 32	..	7 7	...	8 28
7 19	Tetbury .. .... arr.	2507	9 7	11 17	....	1 47	....	5 39	...	7 14	....	8 35

Distance.	**UP TRAINS.** WEEK DAYS.	1	2	3	4	5	6	7	8	9	SUNDAYS.
		Pass.	Pass.			Pass.	Mixed		Pass.		Pass.
M. C.		A.M.	A.M.			NOON.	P.M.		P.M.		P.M.
	Tetbury .. .... dep.	7 40	9 23	....	...	12 20	4 25	....	6 0	...	5 55
2 68	Culkerton .. .. ,,	7 47	9 30	..	...	12 27	4 34	....	6 7	..	6 2
4 16	Rodmarton Platfm ,,	7 50	9 33	....	...	12 30	4 40	....	6 10	....	6 8
6 67	Stop Board ,,	..	..	..	..	..	..	..	..	..	..
7 19	Kemble .... arr.	7 57	9 40	....	...	12 37	4 47	....	6 17	....	6 12

Side lamps not carried on Passenger trains on this Branch.
Engines of 2-4-0 T. type may work over this Branch.

Working timetable 1st January, 1921.

Chapter Five

Fighting for Business

At the beginning of 1921, the weekday passenger service over the branch amounted to eight up and nine down trains, not all of which provided main line connections because the Stroud Valley had not regained its pre-war service levels either. Nor had Sunday trains been restored on the branch. Not only the upheaval of the Great War, but also the high inflation soon after it and the settlement of the 1919 railwaymen's strike, affected the ability of railway companies to reinstate services

Two years later, the Cirencester branch was enjoying ten passenger trains each way on weekdays (but still none Sundays), of which seven up and eight down had Paddington connections.

The year 1923 was the one in which the Grouping of railway companies took effect following the 1921 Railways Act. An enlarged Great Western Railway assumed control of the competing M&SWJ line. The branch terminus, which *Bradshaw* had for years referred to as 'Sheep Street station' to differentiate it from the M&SWJ one, was renamed Cirencester Town from 1st July, 1924, on which date the other station became Cirencester Watermoor, making official a title which *Bradshaw* had already been using.

The latter could not offer a competitive service to London because its own route, to Waterloo via Andover Junction, was 19 miles longer than the GWR route to Paddington and a passenger also travelled a vastly greater mileage before joining a direct train to the capital. So whereas in 1923 the fastest London connection from Cirencester Town departed at 12.35 pm, reaching Paddington at 2.40 pm, the best alternative from Watermoor left at 11.12 am to arrive Waterloo at 2.36 pm. The most vivid contrast was provided by services leaving the two London termini at 7.30 am; the Paddington route provided an arrival in Town station at 10.03 am but a simultaneous departure from Waterloo did not get one to the M&SWJ station until 12.39 pm.

The Depression bites

Passenger and freight traffic remained healthy on the branch until the mid-1920s, whereafter there was a significant decline in passenger numbers and revenue although freight was hardly affected.* As people felt a squeeze on their disposable income particularly after the 10 per cent cut imposed on wages and salaries in 1931, the cheaper fares of Bristol Tramways' buses became a tempting proposition for local travel. In many cases bus services were more direct, particularly to Gloucester (17 miles by road as against 27 by rail via Kemble) and to Stroud. Regular omnibus services from Cirencester to neighbouring towns were well established by 1930.

---

* All traffic statistics in this chapter are quoted from GWR *Annual Traffic Statistics for Stations in the Gloucester Division, 1925-46*, Ref. PRO, Rail 266, (*see Appendix Four for full details*).

Cirencester station throat from near the pig dock, with the goods yard in the distance, 8th June, 1934.   *Mowat Collection/W.R. Burton*

Cirencester station viewed from opposite the goods shed.   *Real Photographs*

The number of passengers booked at Town station was more than halved from 36,546 in 1925 to 16,821 in 1933; annual ticket revenue fell from £10,106 to £4,693 over the same period. Season ticket sales declined in volume though relatively less in terms of income, from 122 issues worth £327 in 1925 to 64 tickets worth £211 in 1930.

The slump in business cannot be blamed entirely on the economic depression because parcels and freight traffic held up well. Cirencester Town forwarded 16,829 parcels in 1925 and received 29,347. Parcels inwards showed healthy growth throughout the 1920s, totalling 38,790 in 1929. The volume of parcels outwards was only slightly down in 1930 at 16,084 although it then began to fall more rapidly to 13,663 in 1934. Total parcels revenue showed a modest rise through the 1920s. Inwards parcels continued to increase during the 1930s, reaching a peak of 61,337 in 1938, when parcels forwarded were only 12,274. Unfortunately the received parcels brought almost nothing to Town station's revenue apart from the occasional excess charge.

One element of railway business at Cirencester Town which practically died out in the mid-1930s was milk carried by passenger train. In 1925 12,780 cans were sent away, earning the GWR £991. Three years later the volume had risen to 14,746 but brought the railway only £956; 1929 saw identical revenue but from 15,862 cans. This suggests the Great Western was having to decrease its rates in the face of road competition and getting a diminishing return. The busiest year was 1930, when 16,530 cans were forwarded from Cirencester Town but income £988 was almost the same as in 1925 despite a 29 per cent increase in containers. Rail business fell sharply in 1931 to 8,809 churns worth £523 before bottoming out at under £100 revenue per year from 1933 onwards. The year 1934 actually saw a nil return for the milk traffic; its resumption in 1935 was at the low level of 251 cans worth £15. Even in 1936, when the station forwarded 1,488 containers, milk netted only £93 receipts.

Freight and livestock traffic

The pattern of freight services in this period was of two or three freight or 'Mixed' trains in each direction on weekdays. 'Mixed' trains tended to be in the down rather than the up direction, wagons arriving off trains such as the 6.00 am Gloucester-Kemble, where it was due at 7.40, in 1921.

Freight business held up remarkably well when one might have expected to see the national slump reflected in reduced carryings. The branch served a mainly agricultural area, less directly affected than were the major manufacturing centres. (Apart from the brewery in Cricklade Street, the most significant local factory closure in this period was of the M&SWJ workshops at Watermoor in 1924.) Freight receipts (other than livestock) at Cirencester Town rose from £28,549 in 1925 to £30,624 in 1927 but then fell steadily to £21,729 in 1932. Yet 1934 witnessed a revival in revenue, thanks to a strong recovery in 'Other Minerals' such as sand and building materials. This boom in freight took off when passenger business was still at a very low ebb; ticket revenue for 1934 at £4,716 was only fractionally above the rock-bottom result of 1933.

Kemble Junction viewed from the Swindon end, with the Cirencester branch on the right, 8th August, 1934.   *Mowat Collection/W.R. Burton*

Geo. Mills & Co. coal wagon, built by the Gloucester Railway Carriage & Wagon Company in October 1935.   *Gloucestershire Record Office/Powell Duffryn*

Goods traffic as a whole would have shown a steady rise from 1933 until 1938 had it not been for a sharp decline in livestock traffic. Livestock wagons forwarded by Town yard slumped from 2,485, worth £8,186 in station revenue, in 1936, to 677, yielding an income of £1,932, in 1937.

In 1921 the cattle market took place on the first Monday of each month and the Cirencester station master had to order an eight-wheel third class carriage for strengthening the branch train on cattle market days, when Tetbury branch stations would offer cheap day tickets to Cirencester after 9.00 am. A special train of cattle wagons was worked empty from Swindon and was due away from Kemble at 11.45 am, reaching the terminus 10 minutes later. The maximum load for this train over the branch was 25 wagons, unless the Cirencester SM could confirm that a heavier load would not delay the midday passenger service.

Ten years later the cattle special, by now serving a twice-monthly market (first and third Mondays), ran to and from Gloucester, working forward empty from Kemble at 11.30 am. No times for the loaded train were shown in the Service Timetable but it is reasonable to assume it was slotted into a suitable gap in the early evening. If traffic was heavy enough to justify another special, the Town station master had to arrange for a locomotive and brake van from Swindon, where this additional train would return with livestock. To cater for visiting farmers, an extra third class carriage was attached to the 10.33 train from Kemble.

A fascinating working in the 1931/32 Winter Timetable was the 4.52 pm Cirencester Town-Swindon 'Mixed' and empty coaching stock (ECS) train, amassing two locomotives, two sets of carriages (those of the 1.58 through train from Swindon plus the regular branch set) and a rake of freight wagons.

The success of the freight business was rewarded with the rebuilding of Cirencester's 97-year-old goods shed in 1938. The old timber building was replaced by a girder structure, of which the roof and much of the sides and ends were covered in cellacite sheeting. The shed platform was given timber extensions of 40 feet at the Kemble end and 60 feet at the north end. One of the two tracks inside the shed was altered to stop short of the shed entrance, to allow more room for lorries.*

The serious loss of passenger business at a time of wage and price inflation dictated economies in station staffing. Annual paybill costs for operating staff at Cirencester Town were around £4,000 throughout this period during which staff numbers shrank from 29 in 1925 to 24 in 1933, although the workforce increased again to 27 in 1935 as freight traffic revived.

The fortunes of Cirencester Town station during the interwar years were largely reflected at Watermoor also. Passengers booked and ticket sales at the ex-M&SWJ station were consistently about half the levels recorded at the Town station; 1927 was a good year for passenger business at both stations. Watermoor also experienced a very steep decline in milk traffic from the 1930s and none is recorded there in GWR statistics after 1934; this suggests that Town continued to send small amounts of milk by passenger train because of its more direct route to the Home Counties via Kemble. Freight tonnage handled at Watermoor during the 1930s was about one third of Cirencester Town's total.

---

* GWR Engineering Plan 65041, date stamped 10.8.38. The contractor's signature, barely legible, appears to read 'Joseph Westwood' and was witnessed by H. Batten, dated 11.7.38.

The Great Western fights back

In the early years of the century it had been the M&SWJ, rather than the GWR, which had used the front page of the *Wilts & Gloucestershire Standard* to promote cheap day and period excursions. But before World War I Great Western advertisements had made a regular appearance, promoting half-day or cheap period return fares, notably to Paddington and Newbury Racecourse. After the war, day return trips were offered to London using the first departure from Cirencester Town around 8 am and to Swindon for football, travelling out at lunchtime. Although there was now less emphasis on the cheap period fares to holiday resorts that had featured in its pre-war publicity, the GWR stepped up the range and frequency of day excursion tickets from Cirencester to meet growing road competition in the 1930s.

The line regained Sunday trains in 1928, though only between early June and the close of the summer timetable in mid-September. Town signal box was opened for a split shift on Sundays (for instance, 1.20-3.45 pm, then 5.25-11 pm in summer 1935) for the running of a round trip just after lunch, enabling people to make half-day trips with a choice of evening trains back, main line connections permitting. Even on its main lines, the Great Western did not provide lavish Sunday services. A case in point was the two-hour wait at Kemble for passengers from London for the first trip down the branch, in July 1939 although this same branch train had an excellent connection into and out of a Cardiff-Gloucester-Paddington semi-fast.

Half-day return tickets to London were available for 6s. 9d. on the 12.30 pm from Cirencester Town in January 1938, when a cheap day return (Mondays, Wednesdays and Saturdays) was offered at 11s. for outward travel on the 8.00 am service. The latter price was actually 6d. lower than the equivalent ticket using the same branch train in 1925.* Also in January 1938, evening trips to Cheltenham were available on two Thursdays when 'Cinderella' was being performed at the Opera House. Outward travel was via the 5.10 pm Cirencester Town, changing at Kemble, and a special connection down the branch brought excursionists back in Town station at 11.30 pm. Both rail-only fares (1s. 10d. adult, 11d. child) and inclusive tickets (3s. extra) were offered.

Sending the theatre-goers the long way round to Cheltenham via Kemble, rather than by a direct train from Watermoor, had probably more to do with the high cost of extending signalmen's hours over the M&SWJ line than with any lingering antipathy of GWR officials to their former rival. Using the Kemble line for evening excursions lengthened the late turn at only one signal box (Cirencester Town); while on Saturdays in 1937-9 the last service train, 11.55 pm from Kemble, would have been late enough anyway. The Great Western did advertise cheap fares from Watermoor where trains filled a gap in what was possible from the Town station; for example a 1s. 4d. Saturday fare to Swindon for football was valid on either the 1.00 pm train from Town or the 1.30 and 2.21 pm services from Watermoor.

Despite the awkward geography of the branch for journeys south-west of Cirencester, the GWR competed keenly with Millers of Cirencester who ran evening coach tours to places such as Bristol and Weston-super-Mare. Unable to offer a direct service, the railway undercut the coach prices with return fares

* *Wilts & Gloucestershire Standard*, 3.1.25, 1.1.38.

such as 2s. 11d. to Bristol and 3s. 2d. to Weston on Easter Sunday, 1938 using a 4.23 pm departure from Town station.

Easter Monday excursion tickets were promoted to Cardiff, Chepstow and Hereford races via the 10.05 am service from Cirencester Town. Among destinations advertised on the Easter Monday and Tuesday were Ledbury (4s. 2d.), Malvern and Worcester (both 4s. 9d.), travelling out on the 8.00 or 11.15 am trains. In July 1939 the 8.00 am train connected into a through Swindon-Newport service, ideal for a day at Chepstow, the Forest of Dean or Wye Valley.

London remained the most heavily promoted long-distance destination for cheap return tickets from Cirencester Town, although the midweek half-day excursions offered only about 3½ hours in the capital. A more varied afternoon could be had by using the same connection (from the 12.30 ex-Cirencester) and alighting at Reading for a combined road and river trip. An attractive package offered on 14th July, 1938 for 8s. 8d. included rail travel to Reading, a visit to Huntley and Palmers biscuit factory, a coach tour, followed by tea and a river cruise before returning to Cirencester by train.

Train services at the outbreak of war

When war broke out, the branch was enjoying its most intensive and possibly most varied service ever. The basic weekday timetable provided 10 up and 11 down trains, with five extra journeys on Saturdays, mainly in the evening. There were two additional trips into Cirencester on Mondays, with a 2.42 pm return service.

There was still a through train between Swindon and Cirencester, running in very similar times to those of 1931/2. The Sunday service had reached its highest point, with seven trains each way, starting with the 1.40 pm from Town station and finishing there just after midnight, allowing a connection to and from the 9.25 Paddington-Neyland. Sunday trains over the branch were operated without a guard, although it was usual to have a ticket examiner on board.

Freight traffic was sufficiently heavy to justify no less than six 'Mixed' trains during the week. Four ran from Kemble in the morning and lunchtime, while the two up 'Mixed' workings at 5.15 and 6.45 pm were also the latest passenger departures from Cirencester. These 'Mixed' trains were over and above the normal freight service consisting of a round trip (5.45 am from Cirencester, 7.10 am from Kemble) preceding the first passenger train, and a 4.25 pm freight from Cirencester returning as a Light Engine and brake van.

The branch in wartime

A National Emergency Timetable came into effect during September 1939* and cut out three round trips from the weekday passenger service as well as removing the Monday extras. Sunday trains were slashed to two trains each way, departures from Cirencester being at 7.40 and 11.20 pm. Town signal box

* *Bradshaw's Railway Guide* No. 1274 (September 1939) shows the passenger trains as in the July Service Timetable. *Bradshaw* No. 1275 (October 1939) shows the reduced service as in the Service Timetable dated 1.12.39.

Signalman Alec Deakins poses inside Cirencester signal box *c.* 1940.   *Frank Deakins Collection*

was now open on weekdays from 5.35 am until after the last train, and on Sundays from 7 to 8.20 pm, then from 11 pm to 12.20 am Monday. The late night Sunday train not only survived these economies but lasted until the branch closed to passengers in 1964.

Another lasting effect of the war was that the Sunday service now ran all year, again right up to 1964. By 1942 the branch was again open on Sunday mornings, this time for special trains conveying RAF personnel and civilian workers to Kemble aerodrome, reached by connecting trains down the Tetbury branch to Jackaments Bridge Halt, which had opened on 3rd July, 1939. Similar trains ran throughout the week and utilised the Tetbury branch auto-train, which ran ECS from Tetbury at 6.00 am, reversing three times at Kemble to gain the Cirencester branch.* The 'RAF Auto' was scheduled to leave Town station at 6.50 am daily, with an additional Sunday departure at 7.50 am. After shunting at Kemble, the auto-train carried its passengers to the new halt and then ran empty to Tetbury. It was also possible to commute to the aerodrome by using the first weekday service train from Cirencester, then at 7.50 am from Cirencester, and changing into an 8.02 am auto-train from Kemble to Jackaments Bridge. Passengers used normal service trains for their journeys home. No reference could be found to these RAF trains in timetables from 1943 onwards, although Jackaments Bridge Halt was not closed until 27th September, 1948.

Passenger traffic reached a peak during the middle of the war. In 1943, Cirencester Town issued 56,446 tickets worth £27,990. Freight also peaked in 1943 for tonnage inwards (44,863) and in 1945 for tonnage outwards (19,117). Both freight and passenger carryings dropped significantly in 1946, although still remaining above the figures of the 1930s.

Accidents

Research has uncovered three accidents on the branch during the war. On 15th January, 1940, G.R. Wheatley, acting carter at Town station, suffered injuries which kept him off work for a month. The GWR paid £6 7s. 3d. compensation.

The most serious accident, involving passenger injuries, occurred when a special cattle train from Cirencester collided with the branch passenger train in the bay at Kemble on Monday 3rd September, 1940. This special would run in the early evening if the regular cattle train, booked to run on the first and third Mondays of each month, could not accommodate all the livestock being dispatched by rail.

The normal procedure was for the livestock trains to be shunted into the loop of the bay platform when the platform line was occupied by the stationary passenger train. It would appear that on this occasion the points had been incorrectly set for the cattle train to run into the bay. When the crew of the livestock special realised a collision was inevitable, they jumped clear although the fireman received slight injuries. The passenger train was driven back by the impact, throwing passengers from their seats.

---

* Auto-trains had a locomotive attached to one or two carriages but could be driven from the windowed carriage end, avoiding the need for the locomotive to run round its train.

Buses replaced the branch train service for the evening and a breakdown gang worked through the night to free the entangled locomotives. Normal working was resumed on the Tuesday morning.*

Rough shunting at Cirencester on 26 January, 1944 was blamed for injuries received by a tradesman, A.H.T. Blackwell, who was working inside a stationary wagon. He was thrown to the floor by the impact, bruising his arm and shoulder. Compensation of £36 5s. 0d. was awarded after the GWR admitted negligence involving a breach of Rule 112a, which required the shunter to ensure that the siding was safe before making a movement. The wagons had been moved into the siding too quickly, causing the shunter to lose control.

Kemble Junction showing the rear of a Cirencester branch train in the bay platform and a freight train in the down main platform, 19th August, 1944.   *D.W. Winkworth*

* *Wilts & Gloucestershire Standard*, 7.9.40.

Chapter Six

The Last Decades of Steam

A Royal visit

The summer 1946 timetable brought improvements to both the frequency of trains on the branch and to the speed of main line expresses. The most impressive service was the down 'Cheltenham Spa Express', which left Paddington at 4.55 pm and was first stop Kemble, where a smart five minute connection reached Cirencester two hours after departure from London. There were seven weekday connections from Paddington to Cirencester Town, of which five involved changing at Kemble only, as against six weekday services from the capital in summer 1943.

The line now enjoyed nine Monday to Friday departures from Cirencester and 10 from Kemble. The 2.45 pm from Cirencester, previously Saturdays only, now ran all week, filling what had been a 3½ hour gap in up trains. The branch regained a late evening train on Saturdays, 10.10 pm from Cirencester, returning from Kemble at 10.50

Just before the new timetable began came news of the King and Queen's visit to the Royal Agricultural College on 22nd May, 1946 to mark its centenary. The original plan had been for the Royal party to leave their train at Kemble, taking cars thence to the college. But the *Wilts & Gloucestershire Standard* of 4th May vented local feeling that such an arrangement would deny Their Majesties the opportunity to see the town or the townspeople the Royal couple. Representations made by the college's Centenary Committee proved successful within days, as the next issue of the *Standard* reported that the Royal Train would steam into Town station at 12.40 pm.

The change of plan enabled the Urban District Councillors to be in attendance at the station and their Chairman, R.A. Berkeley, to be presented to the King. On the appointed day, 200 chairs were placed in front of the old museum, opposite the station forecourt, to give prime viewing for aged and infirm persons. School parties had to be in their allotted positions by 12.15. The *Standard* commented 'Their Majesties will not leave the platform by the somewhat gloomy booking hall but by the side entrance, which will bring them immediately into the station yard'.

The train departed Paddington at 10.10 am, behind 'Castle' class 4-6-0 No. 5056 *Earl of Powis*, which was replaced at Kemble by '45XX' 2-6-2T No. 5506. This tank engine had left Swindon Shed the same morning coupled to sister engine No. 5534. The two 'Prairie' tanks were placed on the Cirencester branch platform line until the Royal Train arrived in the down main platform; No. 5534 then drew the train on to the up main line, ready for No. 5506 to take it forward to Cirencester (*see Appendix Three for further details*).

At Town station the train had to be brought to a stand with the centre of the footplate opposite a white post positioned on the platform. The King and Queen were greeted by the Duke and Duchess of Beaufort, with whom the

'45XX' class 2-6-2T No. 4551 at the head of a branch train, viewed from the Cirencester end of the bay platform at Kemble *c.* 1946.   *Rokeby Collection*

'57XX' class 0-6-0PT No. 4612 awaits departure from Cirencester with a passenger train, probably in the early 1950s.   *Woodfin Collection/Bristol City Museum & Art Gallery*

Royal party were taking tea at Badminton after visiting the college, and by station master C. Feldwick. The Royal cars had arrived the previous day in the station yard, which displayed 'Welcome to Cirencester' in huge gold letters.*

Two round trips of the branch passenger service were replaced by buses in order to keep the section clear for the Royal train. No. 5534 ran light down the branch 20 minutes behind the Royal special in order to work the carriages back to Swindon. When the empty stock had cleared Kemble, No. 5506 ran light to Swindon from Cirencester before working the stock forward to Badminton, whence the train returned to Paddington behind No. 5056 with Their Majesties.

Postwar trends in Passenger Traffic

Just as the line was enjoying a brief high profile, its passenger business began to decline alarmingly. This was due to a decrease in Forces travel and to the easing of petrol rationing, the latter reflected in the resumption of long-distance coach services in June 1946.* Town station had enjoyed a boom in ticket sales during the war, despite a somewhat reduced train service, but tickets issued fell from 48,553 in 1945 to 22,834 in 1948, although remaining steady through the early 1950s (*see Appendix Four*). The ex-M&SWJ station, Cirencester Watermoor, suffered a slower but more certain decline, e.g. from 10,938 tickets sold in 1947 to 5,487 in 1952.

The bright spot of the line's early postwar finances was an upsurge in parcels traffic. Parcels dispatched from Cirencester Town peaked at 19,077 in 1948. These then declined to 15,611 in 1952 but this was similar to the wartime average. The number of parcels arriving at Town station rose from 48,486 in 1947 to 58,191 in 1952 but this would not have been reflected in the station's takings nor, sadly, in the line's accounts when the Beeching proposals were later implemented.

A few weeks after the GWR was nationalised in January 1948, a dinner for local rail staff was held in Viner's Restaurant. Station master Feldwick toasted British Railways, spoke of 'the difficult recent past' and asked people to show 'that little extra cheerfulness which had helped them through darker days.' Mr W.J. Roberts thanked Cirencester's traders for their co-operation; in reply, Mr R.F. McIlroy said he had been glad to meet those who had enabled the railway organisation to work so smoothly.†

Passenger train services

For much of this period, the branch enjoyed a through Swindon train each way. This was provided for stock balancing and locomotive maintenance purposes, although the early afternoon departure from Swindon (1.55 pm in summer 1946) was convenient for returning shoppers. The southbound journey may well have suited people working in Cirencester but living in Minety, Purton or Swindon. This train was often worked by a '45XX' or '51XX' 2-6-2Ts. In winter 1949/50 it left Cirencester at 5.15 pm, forming the 5.25 Kemble-Swindon local.

---

* *Wilts & Gloucestershire Standard*, 25.5.46.
† *ibid.*, 24.1.48.

'57XX' class 0-6-0PT No. 8779 is seen in the bay platform at Kemble having just arrived with the 9.55 am from Cirencester, 6th September, 1952.   *H.C. Casserley*

The same locomotive is seen departing Kemble with the 10.35 am mixed train to Cirencester a little later in the day.   *H.C. Casserley*

In the 1950s, the pattern was of 10 trains each way Mondays to Fridays, with one or two extra on Saturdays, and a 12.05 am from Kemble on Monday mornings, connecting out of the Paddington-Neyland sleeper.   Three other Sunday trains from Kemble plus this midnight working were balanced by four services from Cirencester but no Sunday trains ran before early evenings - in winter 1951/2 the first was 6.20 pm from Cirencester.

The enhanced Saturday passenger service was influenced by the lesser requirements of the freight service at weekends. In winter 1951/2 there was a 5.30 pm Saturday departure from Kemble, but during the week this slot was taken up by a light engine and brake van balancing the 4 pm freight from Cirencester. This suggests that the engine and brake van crossed at Kemble with the 5.15 pm Cirencester-Swindon passenger train; also that the latter terminated at Kemble on Saturdays in order to return as the 5.30 pm to Cirencester.

The late evening train on Saturdays catered for cinema visits and dovetailed at Kemble with main line trains to create a series of connections. It was possible to return to Cirencester from either the Stroud or Swindon directions by using trains that connected into the last trip down the branch (the 10.50 pm from Kemble). An essential link in this chain was the Saturday extension to Kemble of the last Gloucester-Chalford auto-train.

The advertised connection from Cirencester into the up 'Cheltenham Spa Express' was not a train at all but was the 8.24 am Bristol Tramways bus from Town station forecourt. This was because the earliest train up the branch left Town station about an hour before the express left Kemble. The timing of the first branch train was a compromise aimed at connecting into a train for Gloucester and a slower London train running ahead of the 'Cheltenham Spa Express'.

Two railways at cross-purposes?

Town was very much Cirencester's main station by now, for arguably the only superior services at Watermoor were the direct (though sparse) trains to Southampton and Cheltenham Lansdown, where some useful northward connections existed. The M&SWJ line also filled some gaps in services between Cirencester Town and Swindon, but became a less feasible alternative when its timetable was slashed by the cuts of 30th June, 1958.

Watermoor had ceased to be a viable station for London journeys by the early 1950s. It now had few Waterloo connections via Andover, while a Watermoor-Paddington trip normally involved changing at both Swindon Town and Swindon Junction. As late as 1949 it was still possible to catch the 6.34 am from Watermoor, then a through train to Savernake, where there was a convenient connection into a Trowbridge-Paddington service. But by 1952 the 6.34 am from Watermoor went no further than Swindon Town.

More could have been done to exploit the complementary role of Cirencester's two stations in meeting the town's travel needs, for instance by advertising tickets as available by either route to certain destinations. This was

A view at Cirencester along the platform looking towards the buffer stops, showing the stock of a mixed train and the station buildings, 6th September, 1952.   *R.M. Casserley*

'57XX' class 0-6-0PT No. 8779 is seen near Ewen with the 11.52 am from Kemble, 2nd June, 1954.
Hugh Ballantyne

indeed done to promote off peak travel to Swindon; in summer 1956 cheap day fares of 2s. 6d. were available to Swindon from either station every day. The absence of Sunday trains from Watermoor was partly compensated for by the running of a late morning train from Town to Kemble on specific Sundays and advertised locally as a Cheltenham connection. But the cheap day fare was 4s. 3d., compared with 3s. on a weekday lunchtime train from Watermoor, reflecting rail distances of 20 miles via the M&SWJ route and 34 via Kemble and Gloucester.

One apparently missed opportunity for exploiting both railways at Cirencester was Swindon commuter traffic. The first weekday departure from Town station connected into the 7.10 am Cheltenham St James, due Swindon at 8.41 am (in the winter 1952/3 timetable) but for years there was no satisfactory return service by the Kemble route for people working normal office hours. Yet the 5.45 pm Swindon Town-Cirencester Watermoor, due there at 6.15, seemed the ideal train home.

Melvin Hatch, who often covered Cirencester Town booking office as a Bristol district relief clerk during this period, cannot recall a ticket being actually routed for outward travel from Town and return from Watermoor or vice versa. John Thomas remembers people travelling out by one route and returning the other but stresses that this was down to their local knowledge.

Alarm Signals

Public confidence in the future of both Cirencester stations was undermined in June 1956 by the abrupt termination of rebuilding work on the main building at Town station that had begun only a few months previously. It was not so much the unfinished work, as the accompanying statement that the line's future was under review, that hit the local headlines.

British Railways had been reviewing the future of branch lines for several years in the wake of worsening finances, and particularly since the 1953 Transport Act which had untied many of the restrictions on road haulage. There had been passenger closures locally: Culkerton station on the Tetbury branch as recently as March 1956; the Highworth branch in 1953 and the Malmesbury branch in 1951. But these stations had been very little used by comparison with Cirencester Town, which was now estimated to have a daily average of 200 passengers. This and the fact that the £9,000 modernisation work was nearly finished must have looked particularly ominous.

A Public Relations Officer at Paddington disclosed to the local press that an Investigation Committee had turned its attention to the branch; hence the decision to suspend work on the project. He said this did not mean the passenger service was definitely going to be withdrawn but that rebuilding work might have to be modified in the light of the Committee's eventual decision.*

To have even admitted that the line was a possible candidate for closure at a time when a significant investment in the station was nearing completion, was a public relations own-goal. Local people may well have formed a strong

* *Wilts & Gloucestershire Standard*, 23.6.56.

'57XX' class 0-6-0PT No. 7792 arrives at Cirencester with the 10.35 am from Kemble, bunker first on 1st May, 1956. Note the cattle wagons to the right.   *H.C. Casserley*

The same locomotive is seen at the platform buffers prior to running round its train. Horse boxes are seen to the left, 1st May, 1956.   *H.C. Casserley*

'57XX' class 0-6-0PT No. 3739 runs round its passenger train at Cirencester. Scaffolding on the roof suggests the date as 1956.   *David Lawrence*

No. 3739 now stands ready for departure from Cirencester.   *David Lawrence*

'57XX' class 0-6-0PT No. 7794 on shed at Cirencester *c.* 1956.   *C.L. Caddy Collection*

'45XX' class 2-6-2T No. 4538 on arrival at Cirencester with a two-coach train from Kemble *c.* 1956.   *C.L. Caddy Collection*

impression of a railway management lacking unity of purpose. Coming a year after the ASLEF (footplate staff) strike, when the nation had been surprised by its ability to cope without trains for 17 days, this clumsy disclosure may well have fuelled speculation that Cirencester might not always have a railway.

Freight traffic

The same press article which speculated on whether Town station would remain open for passenger services was confident that its freight and parcels traffics were sufficiently heavy to continue into the foreseeable future. For at that time Town goods yard had a crane of 12 tons capacity, equalling those at Cheltenham St James and Swindon; none of Gloucester's goods yards then had a crane more powerful than 10 tons while the ex-GWR goods yard at Stroud could only boast a 6 tons crane. The lion's share of freight traffic at Cirencester was handled via Town station as Watermoor was by then dealing only in coal class traffic in full truck loads and had no crane.

The main inward cargoes, not surprisingly for a sizeable country town, were coal, timber and farm feedstuffs. The coal sidings served five local merchants. Messrs Hucks were the local distributors for Bibby's of Liverpool who sent cattle cake to Cirencester. Also receiving traffic by rail was local corn and forest merchant John Smith.

Livestock traffic was heavy enough to justify two loading docks. Jim Biggs, who worked at Cirencester as a shunter from 1942-57, recalls that the annual cattle fair generated an order for 30 wagons. Cirencester sheep fair also provided a peak of traffic during the war and early post-war years. Brian Carter recalls helping a local farmer unload sheep and drive them along the lane from the station. He remembers one occasion when a 'Dean Goods' 0-6-0 worked a special freight train, there being three locomotives on the branch at the time. Jim Biggs has recalled particularly busy days when one engine was shunting at Cirencester Town, one was on shed there and another was in the Cirencester-Kemble section:

> Live pigs for the bacon factories of Messrs Cole & Lewis, Mason & Gillett and the Danish Bacon Company were a regular inward cargo; these firms also exported their produce by rail. Being a perishable cargo, bacon was given a high priority for dispatch. Bill Roberts, who worked at Cirencester Town from 1937-60, recalls busy 'bacon days' when he would come on duty at 8 am but often remain at work beyond his rostered booking-off time of 5 pm. He remembers five or six tons of bacon arriving at the station on a typical 'bacon day'. Regular destinations for the bacon included London, Manchester, Cardiff and Newport.

If the loads were not ready to be forwarded by the afternoon freight service to Kemble (4.00 pm from Cirencester in September 1951), they had to be dispatched by the early morning freight which preceded the first up passenger train. In September 1951 this freight was scheduled to leave Cirencester at 5.45 am, 10 minutes after the signal box opened, and to return from Kemble at 7.10, arriving back at 7.23 am. The apparently generous time allowance for the out and back trip was to encompass shunting at Kemble; Jim Biggs has recalled the train arriving with up to 30 wagons at Cirencester.

'Castle' class 4-6-0 No. 5017 *The Gloucestershire Regiment 28th, 61st* enters Kemble station with the down 'Cheltenham Spa Express' while '57XX' class 0-6-0PT No. 9720 prepares to run round the Cirencester branch train in 1957.   *P.J. Sharpe*

'57XX' class 0-6-0PT No. 9740 arrives at Cirencester with a two-coach train from Kemble *c*. 1957.
P.J. Sharpe

Mixed Trains

Until the mid-1950s the first down passenger train (8.45 am from Kemble) sometimes had as many as 20 wagons in tow. 'Mixed' trains were still a fairly common feature of ex-GWR branches in early BR days and were a useful means of getting urgent cargoes to a main line. In the winter 1951/2 timetable there were three 'mixed' trains on weekdays from Kemble at 10.35 am, 11.52 am and 1.10 pm, compared with one back from Cirencester at 7.45 pm. The tendency to send freight up the branch in normal freight trains and down it in 'mixed' trains was probably dictated by marshalling requirements. Cirencester Town's yard was larger than Kemble's and there was no conflict with main line trains when shunting at the branch terminus.

The ruling gradient also favoured longer trains up the branch than down it. In 1951 Group 'A' engines such as '16XX', '20XX' and '74XX' pannier tanks were allowed loads not exceeding 40 wagons from Kemble for a Class 1 train and 48 wagons for a Class 2 train. The corresponding maxima from Cirencester were 45 and 54 wagons. For empty wagons the maximum permitted load was 60 in either direction. 'Mixed' trains were timed to cover the branch in 11 minutes, compared with eight minutes for passenger and 10-13 minutes for freight trains.*

Freight Resources

The Early Turn shunter's hours were based on the arrival and departure at Cirencester of the two key freight trains, the 7.10 am Kemble and the 4 pm Cirencester. The former was naturally geared to shop and market deliveries. In the 1940s and 1950s the shunter came on duty at 7.15 am and normally worked through to 3.15 pm, assisted by the station foreman chasing wagons with a brake stick.

In the early postwar years Cirencester Town had more freight staff than passenger staff, not only because freight traffic was heavy but probably also because the passenger station was a compact one-platform affair. Whereas the passenger staff comprised the station master, two parcels porters, two platform porters and a horse carman (latterly a lorry driver), the Goods Department boasted six porters, an inwards Checker, Empty Wagons Checker and two lorry drivers for town deliveries. Additionally there were four lorry rounds delivering to rural areas such as Fairford, Minety, South Cerney and Tetbury whose local stations did not cater for traffic in less than full wagon loads. The lorry rounds also made bulk deliveries of fertiliser and animal feedstuffs to outlying farms.

Jim Biggs believes the branch was a 'very paying concern' in terms of tonnage per mile and one of the most profitable branch lines in the Bristol Traffic District in early BR days. But freight was to decline to the extent that by 1958 there was just one 'mixed' train each way - 10.25 am ex-Kemble and 7.45 pm ex-Cirencester. These ceased by the time the passenger service was dieselised in 1959, when one daily freight sufficed for the traffic. This decline was attributed

* BR Western Region Service Timetable commencing 14.9.51.

'57XX' class 0-6-0PT No. 9772 passes through Cirencester station's throat as it leaves with a passenger train for Kemble bunker first *c*. 1958.   *R.E. Toop*

No. 9772 as it approaches Kemble bunker first with the branch train *c*. 1958.   *R.E. Toop*

to the proliferation of heavier lorries which could take loads such as fertiliser from Liverpool docks direct to the farms.

Yet BR did make the effort to sell itself to freight customers and increase the efficiency of its service. From the mid-1950s freight consignments of less than a full wagonload were concentrated on a strategic network of depots including Cirencester Town as a satellite of a main railhead for the area at Swindon.* The aim of this policy was to speed up transit by a combination of fewer depots and wider scale road collection and delivery, not yet carried to an extreme position as it was to be under the Beeching Plan.

Shortly after the branch passenger service was dieselised, the line was the spotlight of an excellent press publicity feature for contemporary rail freight at its best. An article headed 'Express rail freight aids farmers' described how 240 tons of fertiliser left by special train from ICI Billingham at 2.20 pm on a Monday and was ready for unloading at Cirencester Town at 3 pm Tuesday. Normal rail transit times for this journey of 260 miles were quoted as three to seven days. The train had been run for the benefit of local farmers hoping to make the most of favourable weather - a very businesslike response by both parties. Special freight workings of this kind were said to require a minimum load of 200 tons to be viable. The article described this train as an express service that BR would introduce generally as soon as the necessary modifications (i.e. automatic brakes) could be fitted to the wagon fleet.†

As things turned out, it was to be well into the 1970s, a decade after the line closed, before BR had a sizeable fleet of air braked, long-wheelbase wagons for bulk fertiliser traffic.

Locomotives and train crews

Ray Keylock trained as a fireman at Gloucester from 1943-5 and came to Cirencester as a passed fireman in November 1945, remaining there until the branch passenger service was dieselised in 1959. He recalls that two drivers and two fireman were based at Cirencester until then.

The early turn driver worked 4.45 am to 1.35 pm; his first trip along the branch was the early morning freight, which might only comprise an engine and brake van if all loaded wagons had been dispatched from Cirencester the previous day. One of the reasons for this early trip was to collect a shunter based at Kemble and who worked at Cirencester as well. He travelled down the branch with the 7.10 am freight from Kemble.

On late turn the driver worked from 1.30 to 9.30 pm, except on Saturdays when the shift finished at 11.00 pm because of the additional passenger train on the branch. Sunday duty was from 6.00 pm - 20 minutes before the first train - until after the last train (12.05 am Monday) had been berthed at Cirencester and the engine was back on shed.

Relief footplate crews came from Gloucester Horton Road, of which Cirencester was then a sub-shed If the early turn at Cirencester was vacant, the

* The statutory notice confirming the closure of Culkerton station, on the Tetbury branch, announced that 'existing arrangements for collection and delivery of smalls and parcels traffic at Cirencester Town will continue'.
† *Wilts & Gloucestershire Standard*, 7.2.59.

'4575' class 2-6-2T No. 5547 is seen as it runs round the Cirencester branch train at Kemble, 24th
April, 1958.   *H.C. Casserley*

'28XX' class 2-8-0 No. 2870 is seen on an up main freight through Kemble. No. 5547 can just be
seen as it stands in readiness with the Cirencester branch train in the bay platfrom, 24th April,
1958.   *H.C. Casserley*

resident late turn driver would work the early shift so that the relief man could cover the late turn. Ray Keylock sometimes used to work spare driver's turns on the Tetbury branch.

A peculiarity of the arrangements for Cirencester shed was that although relief staff were supplied from Gloucester, its locomotives were supplied by Swindon.* This was probably influenced by railway geography and the compatibility of branch locomotive with the rolling stock used for Swindon-Kemble shuttle trains. To have supplied engines from Gloucester would have either involved lengthy light engine movements or else revamping the Chalford auto-trains to serve Kemble; in any case many of the locomotive types shedded at Cirencester were not auto-fitted.

Denzil Rees remembers relieving firemen's turns at Cirencester when he was based at Horton Road. The limitations of the train service made it normal practice for the resident Cirencester fireman to work the early turn while the late turn was covered by the relief man, who booked on duty about 4 pm in order to travel to Cirencester.

Firing at Cirencester did not afford the luxury of having other depot staff to drop the fire after the engine had completed its work for the day as was the case at Horton Road and other large ex-GWR depots. Denzil Rees recalls that when the engine of the last branch train had been berthed at Cirencester, he would spend an hour or so dropping the fire and refilling the tanks before taking a taxi to Kemble, returning to Gloucester on a down postal train.

If a driver's duty was uncovered at Cirencester, it was usual for his fireman to cover for him with the firing turn being relieved from Gloucester.

The resident locomotive at Cirencester tended to be a '57XX' 0-6-0PT, although the lighter '64XX' and '74XX' varieties were also seen on passenger duties. Class '45XX' 2-6-2Ts were allowed on the branch but were originally barred from the shed because they would foul the smoke troughs. Hence their use on the Swindon through train which did not require its engine to remain overnight at Cirencester. Colin Maggs has commented that the troughs were later raised to overcome this problem, although the Working Timetable for winter 1960/1 still specified this restriction. Some of the last class '850' 0-6-0PTs, rebuilt from saddle tanks, used the line, among them No. 2014 which was reinstated in service at Cirencester in 1940. It was withdrawn finally at Swindon in November 1951, having been built originally in 1894.†

The working timetable for September 1951 quotes standard loads for passenger trains on the branch by groups of engine classes. Engines in the 'A' Group (listed as '16XX', '19XX', '20XX', '21XX' and '74XX' all pannier tanks - plus 'Dean Goods' 0-6-0s) were permitted to take up to 280 tons from Kemble and 300 tons from Cirencester. 0-4-2 tanks in classes '14XX' and '58XX' were authorised to haul 252 tons from Kemble and 280 from Cirencester, as in theory were class '517' 2-4-0 tanks which hardly survived into BR ownership.

* R. Griffiths, GWR *Sheds in Camera*, Oxford Publishing Company.
† J.W.P. Rowledge, GWR *Locomotive Allocations*, David and Charles.

Front cover for the timetable commencing 2nd February, 1959
complete with an illustration of one of the railbuses.

Chapter Seven

The Reign of the Railbus

Why railbuses from Kemble?

The two branches from Kemble were chosen to be the Western Region's testbed for one of the more memorable features of BR's 1955 Modernisation Plan. The Plan envisaged that no more steam locomotives would be built after 1960 and that manufacture of diesel trains would be contracted out to a variety of firms as well as BR itself.

The ideal train for short distance rural services was considered to be a lightweight short wheelbase one-carriage diesel railbus based on extensive Continental practice. The aim was to save on fuel, track maintenance and on labour because no fireman was needed in the cab, although a guard was still required to collect fares and for the overall safety of the train. The inference was that with Government pressure on BR to reduce the losses it had been incurring each year since 1953, more economic methods of operation *might well* enable lines to continue offering passenger services that could not be run economically either with steam or with more commodious diesel trains.

The emphasis was on *'might well'* rather than an actual commitment to keeping the lines open. The experiment was cautious and limited to a few lines in four regions - a 'wait and see' approach based on a mixture of technological innovation, cost-cutting and more vigorous marketing. This seems a thoughtful response of the railways to a political climate not particularly favourable to them.*

While it was operationally convenient to link railbus operation on the Cirencester branch with that to Tetbury the choice may have been made out of a desire to allay the suspicions created by the station rebuilding fiasco. After all other pairs of branches would seem to have been feasible candidates; for instance the two branches from Kingham or from Tiverton Junction. A more cynical explanation is that an enhanced service on the Cirencester Town branch might attract passengers from the M&SWJ line which the WR Management wished to close.

The Vehicles

Contracts were placed in May 1957 with five manufacturers to supply railbuses to BR and the first to materialise were produced by Associated Commercial Cars at their works in Thames Ditton, Surrey. This firm, formerly known as Auto-Carriers, was making its debut in railway engineering, being better known for its sports cars and invalid tricycles. Its prototype railbus was delivered to the Western Region in February 1958, tested and promptly transferred to Scotland to

---

* A few weeks before the railbuses entered service, Earl Bathurst had told Cirencester Young Conservatives that one of the chief problems in Britain was the 'appalling losses made by nationalised industries'. (*Wilts & Gloucestershire Standard*, 17.1.59.)

KEMBLE — CIRENCESTER
SECOND CLASS ONLY

WEEKDAYS

	a.m.	a.m.	a.m.	a.m.	a.m. S	a.m.	p.m.	p.m.	p.m.	p.m.
London (Paddington) dep	5 30	7 30	9 5	10 5	11 5			2 15		
Kemble dep	8 30	9 20	10 10	11 20	12P45	1P18	2 35	3 25	3 25	
Chesterton Lane Halt dep	8 38	9 28	10 18	11 28	12 53	1 26	2 43	3 33		
Cirencester (Town) arr	8 41	9 31	10 21	11 31	12 56	1 29	2 46	3 36		

SUNDAYS

	p.m.	p.m.	p.m.	p.m. E	p.m. S	p.m.	p.m. s	p.m.	p.m.	p.m.	Night 9P25
London (Paddington) dep	4 55				6 35	7 15					
Kemble dep	5 5	5 38	6 38	7 7	7 15	8 8	8 42	10 35	6 43	7 55	8 47 12 5
Chesterton Lane Halt dep	5 13	5 46	6 46	7 15	7 23	8 16	8 50	10 43	6 51	8 3	8 55 12 13
Cirencester (Town) arr	5 16	5 49	6 49	7 18	7 25	8 19	8 53	10 46	6 54	8 6	8 58 12 17

On Sundays Bristol Omnibus Co., Ltd. buses leave Kemble Station at 2.0 p.m. and 3.45 p.m. and arrive Cirencester (Town Station) at 2.15 p.m. and 4.0 p.m. respectively. Buses also leave Cirencester (Town Station) at 1.30 p.m. and 3.15 p.m. and arrive Kemble Station at 1.45 p.m. and 3.30 p.m., respectively.

KEMBLE — TETBURY
WEEKDAYS ONLY — SECOND CLASS ONLY

	a.m.	a.m.	a.m.	a.m. S	p.m.	p.m.	p.m.	p.m.	p.m.	p.m.
London (Paddington) dep	5 30	7 30	9 5	11 5		2 15		4 55	6 35	
Kemble dep	8 35	10 10	11 55	1P20	2 40	4 13	5 10	6 55	8 50	
Rodmarton Pform. dep	8 41	10 16	12P1	1 26	2 46	4 19	5 16	7 4	8 56	
Church's Hill Halt dep	8 44	10 19	12 4	1 29	2 49	4 22	5 19	7 7	9 0	
Culkerton Halt dep	8 47	10 22	12 7	1 32	2 52	4 25	5 22	7 9	9 0	
Trouble House Halt dep	8 51	10 26	12 11	1 36	2 56	4 29	5 26	7 11	9 8	
Tetbury arr	8 58	10 33	12 18	1 43	3 3	4 36	5 33	7 18	9 15	

	a.m.	a.m.	a.m.	p.m.	p.m. S	p.m.	p.m.	p.m.	p.m.	
Tetbury dep	7 50	9 17	10 40	12 25	2 5	3 45	4 44	6 5	7 39	
Trouble House Halt dep	7 53	9 20	10 43	12 28	2 8	3 48	4 47	6 8	7 42	
Culkerton Halt dep	7 57	9 24	10 47	12 32	2 12	3 52	4 51	6 12	7 46	
Church's Hill Halt dep	8 0	9 27	10 50	12 35	2 15	3 55	4 54	6 15	7 49	
Rodmarton Pform. dep	8 3	9 30	10 53	12 38	2 18	3 58	4 57	6 18	7 52	
Kemble arr	8 7	9 34	11	12 47	2 27	4	5 6	6 27	8 1	
London (Paddington) arr	8 12	9 39	11 2	12P15	3 0	5 35	6 55	8 5	9 25	10 50

S — Saturdays only.   E — Except Saturdays.

Times in red in the above Tables indicate services operated by Diesel Railbus (Second Class only)

P = p.m.

SPECIAL CHEAP DAY RETURN TICKETS

Issued daily, between the undermentioned places, for travel outward and return by any train the same day. Children under 3 years of age — free; 3 years and under 14 years of age — half fare.

SEASON TICKETS

Season Tickets are issued permitting unlimited travel between the stations selected, for any period from one to twelve months, or for odd periods, e.g., one month and nine days.

Weekly Season Tickets are issued for distances not exceeding 75 miles and are available for an unlimited number of journeys from Sunday to Saturday inclusive.

FARES AVAILABLE IN EACH DIRECTION

SECOND CLASS

	Swindon s. d.	Kemble s. d.	Rodmarton Platform s. d.	Church's Hill Halt s. d.	Culkerton Halt s. d.	Trouble House Halt s. d.	Tetbury s. d.	Chesterton Lane Halt s. d.
Kemble	2 10							
Rodmarton Platform	3 0	9						
Church's Hill Halt	3 0	10	4					
Culkerton Halt	3 1	11	6	4				
Trouble House Halt	3 4	1 3	8	6	4			
Tetbury	3 6	1 6	11	9	8	6		
Chesterton Lane Halt	2 11	11	1 5	1 6	1 9	1 11	2 3	
Cirencester (Town)	3 0	1 0	1 6	1 8	1 10	2 0	2 2	5 3

NOTICE AS TO CONDITIONS. These tickets are issued subject to the British Transport Commission's published Regulations and Conditions applicable to British Railways exhibited at their Stations or obtainable free of charge at Station Booking Offices. The train services and other facilities shown in this publication are subject to alteration or cancellation. Further information will be supplied on application to Stations, Agencies, or to Mr. M. G. Cooper, District Commercial Manager, Northgate Mansions, Gloucester (Telephone: Gloucester 21121, Extension 83); or to Mr. E. Flaxman, Commercial Officer, Paddington Station, W.2.

Paddington Station, W.2.
January, 1959

K. W. C. GRAND
General Manager

Timetable commencing 2nd February, 1959.

work the Gleneagles-Comrie branch. Production of the other four, destined for Western Region, was delayed by a fire at the A.C. Cars premises but the second vehicle underwent trials on the Tetbury branch in August of that year at the same time as a new single railcar, No. W55018, built by Gloucester Railway Carriage & Wagon Works, was being tested over the Cirencester branch.*

Ironically the latter type of diesel unit, still in service in 1994, had 19 more seats per vehicle than the railbuses; with other advantages such as greater parcels space and the ability to operate on track-circuited main lines, the bogie railcars would have been a better choice of rolling stock for the Cirencester branch but the decision was made to operate both routes with railbuses. Usage of the Tetbury branch may not have justified a larger vehicle and there was an opportunity to utilise the small fleet of Swindon-based railbuses more cheaply if the workload was limited to two adjacent routes.

In common with most other British railbuses, the A.C. Cars vehicles had no conventional buffers. In place of buffers were a pair of rounded brackets with lamp iron; this structure was attached to the body subframe rather than to the underframe. These brackets were not intended to cope with the stress of shunting but rather as a means of towing the vehicle should a breakdown occur. Nor could they haul trailers or run in multiple, which suggests that the criterion for selecting railbus routes was a minimal seasonal variation in traffic. Tourism was much less important in the Cotswolds in the 1950s than it is today.

Basic dimensions of the A.C. Cars train included a tare weight of 11 tons; length over buffers 37 ft; wheelbase 19 ft; wheel diameter 3 ft; overall height above rail a little over 12 ft; and width over panels almost 9 ft. The vehicle was powered by a single British United Traction six-cylinder horizontal engine with mechanical transmission. Forty-six seats were provided (second class only) in two saloons which each had a central gangway and were separated by a centre vestibule. Two air-operated sliding doors were controlled by the driver and slid into pockets in the body frame. Release cocks near the doors both inside and outside the vehicle catered for emergencies and for traincrews to enter as this type of railbus had no cab doors. If this was not sufficient incentive for railbus crews to like their passengers, there was also a curved seat for three people next to the cab which was in the left corner of each end.

At one end of the underframe was a 50 gallon fuel tank. The roof, cab ends and cab windows were more rounded than on the Park Royal railbuses used on the LM and Scottish Regions.

Marketing and Publicity

Excursion fares from Cirencester Town were already being vigorously promoted before the railbuses took over the service. In January 1959 Saturday trips to Swindon football matches were being advertised at 2s. 10d. return, travelling out by the 12.35 or 12.59 pm departures; this was exploiting the advantages of the Kemble connection because not only did Town have more trains than Watermoor station but Swindon Junction was also much nearer to the football ground than was the ex-M&SWJ station in Swindon's Old Town.

* *Railway Observer*, October 1958. The date quoted is 19.8.58.

Railbus No. W79977 stands in the Tetbury bay at Kemble. Note the large water tank and signal box beyond. *T.J. Saunders*

A railbus stands at Cirencester station on 20th February, 1960. *Edwin Wilmhurst*

Also in evidence were cheap trips to Cirencester on Mondays, Fridays and Saturdays from Tetbury (2s. return), Oaksey Halt, Minety and Purton using lunchtime or early afternoon trains for the outward journey. Every weekday except Mondays and Fridays there were cheap day returns to Reading (12s. 6d.) and Paddington (£1) using the 8.05 or 9.40 am trains from Cirencester. Arguably the launch of railbus operation served to highlight the bargain fares rather than the other way round. By contrast, since the late 1980s introduction of 'state of the art' rolling stock in rural areas has been given as the reason for fare *increases* said to be needed to pay for the investment. But in summer 1961, over two years after the start of railbus working, the Reading and London cheap day fares from Cirencester had remained virtually the same as in 1959.

By today's standards the advance publicity for the railbuses was modest and straightforward, without any trace of media 'hype'. The first feature in the *Wilts & Gloucestershire Standard* was on 24th January, 1959, just nine days before the new service began. Commenting that 40 of the 46 seats in the railbus faced longways, the *Standard* praised the 'clear view of the track and surrounding countryside' afforded by this arrangement. Other plus points noted by the article were the more intensive service on both branches - in Cirencester's case an extra four trains to Kemble on weekdays - and the cheap day tickets available between local stations and halts. It was not only the lower running costs of railbuses compared with steam traction, but also their quicker turn-round times, that enabled a more frequent service to be provided. Arguably this more than compensated for the actual journey over the branch taking three minutes longer than with steam power.

The first railbus journeys on Monday 2nd February, 1959 received television coverage and a leading article and photograph in the *Standard*. The newspaper remarked that the dieselised service 'is in the nature of an experiment, on the success of which may depend the fate of many smaller branch lines'.

The last regular steam passenger service, had left Cirencester Town at 11.30 pm on the previous Sunday hauled by 0-6-0PT No. 9672, crewed by driver W.T. Timbrell and fireman G. Godsell. Mr Timbrell had started his career with the GWR at Tyseley in 1917, later working at Fairford and Llantrisant before moving to Cirencester in 1949. He retired at the end of 1962.

Unlike the corresponding event at Tetbury on the Saturday, when mourners and a skiffle group were out in force, the last scheduled steam passenger train from Cirencester Town appears to have had no ceremony. The railbus now occupied the engine shed, making fireman Ray Keylock surplus to requirements there; he transferred to Swindon before leaving the industry later that year.

In another break with railway tradition, the railbuses were among the first trains on British Railways to employ conductor guards, who issued tickets from Setright machines. Cheap day return tickets to Cirencester, Kemble, Swindon and Tetbury were now available from all stations bounded by these four points. They were valid to Cirencester by any train, any day. Fares included Kemble-Cirencester 1s., Tetbury-Cirencester 2s. 2d. (but 2s. 5d. vice versa) and 3d. to Cirencester from the new Chesterton Lane Halt which opened with the new service.

The provision of halts on the two branches was in keeping with a tradition of providing basic stopping places in locations which would not justify a substantially built station. Chesterton Lane Halt, located at 94 miles 49 chains from Paddington (47 chains south of Cirencester Town) represented a new generation of very basic stations which were more spartan even than the halts provided when railmotor and auto-train services were developed, as in the Stroud Valley, earlier in the century. Unlike the earlier halts served by auto-trains, Chesterton Lane had no shelter and was at rail height because the railbuses had retractable steps. Moreover, it was only long enough to accommodate a one-coach train. The basic design was for a platform 25 ft long and 8 ft 6 in. wide, constructed from old sleepers.* Vera Pope, the Ewen housewife who was to spearhead the fight to save the line from the Beeching cuts, has referred to the halts as consisting of 22 parallel sleepers fixed together with six sleepers as cross bracing.†

BR was now placing extra weekly columns in the *Wilts and Gloucestershire Standard* featuring a silhouette of the railbus along with a route diagram and fares. The publicity campaign was successful, at least in terms of passenger volume. Within six weeks of the diesel service commencing, BR's assistant district commercial manager, D. Foster, told a local railwaymen's social evening that the railbuses had generated a great increase in the number of shoppers coming from Tetbury to Cirencester by train. The Gloucester-based manager described the new trains as 'a real attempt to keep a reasonable passenger service on both branches'.# From 28th March two additional Saturday journeys were provided; the 2.35 pm Kemble-Cirencester thereafter ran Mondays to Fridays, being replaced on Saturdays by 2.16 pm and 2.40 pm departures.

The more favourable economics of railbus passenger services, compared with steam operation, impressed councillors in neighbouring Malmesbury who now argued for the reopening of their branch line to Little Somerford which had lost its passenger service in 1951.

Probably the greatest single improvement that the railbuses brought to the Cirencester branch timetable was the additional weekday departure from Town station at 8.45 am, connecting smartly into the up 'Cheltenham Spa Express'. Now that one could leave Cirencester 40 minutes later by train than before to achieve the same arrival time in London, the branch was a more attractive proposition for the day return market; Town station master Charles Beard reported in the first week of railbus operation that several businessmen were catching this 8.45 service who had hitherto driven to Kemble for the London train.

There was no longer any advantage to through rail passengers in using the 8.24 am bus from Town station forecourt; this now ceased to be advertised in the BR timetable. Sunday afternoon buses still featured in the branch table footnotes and through Ordinary single and return rail tickets continued to be valid on these Sunday buses as the line remained shut until early evening. The absence of Sunday morning trains may well have been a commercial mistake, at

---

* Dimensions quoted by J.M. Tolson, 'End of an Experiment', Railway Magazine, October 1964.
† *Wilts & Gloucestershire Standard*, 26.7.63.
# *Wilts & Gloucestershire Standard*, 21.3.59.

least in summer when there was most scope for day trip business. But a better Sunday service would have required an additional shift at Cirencester Town signal box, at an enhanced rate of pay.

Overall the first railbus timetable provided 13 trains each way Mondays to Fridays and 16 on Saturdays. The 5.20 pm Cirencester and 5.38 pm Kemble, previously Saturdays only, now ran each weekday. One journey each way (3.50 pm Cirencester and 4.25 pm Kemble) disappeared with the end of steam haulage but another pair of afternoon trains (3.22 pm Kemble and 3.40 pm Cirencester) was introduced with the opening of Park Leaze Halt on 4th January, 1960. This further boost to the branch now gave it 17 trains each way on Saturdays, 14 on other weekdays.

Park Leaze Halt, sited 1½ miles from Kemble at 92 miles 47 chains, served Ewen village and a collection of farms; its construction was similar to Chesterton Lane Halt. Railbuses were now allowed an extra minute to traverse the branch; presumably this was to accommodate the lowering and raising of the vehicle steps. The year 1960 was perhaps the high point of the railbus service and the additional Saturday trains were aimed at relieving overcrowding.

Working the service

An essential feature of the railbus operation was the interlinked diagram involving the two branches from Kemble. One railbus was stabled overnight in the engine shed at each branch terminus. Every weekday morning the Tetbury railbus transferred to the Cirencester branch and its sister vehicle from Cirencester ran empty to Swindon for servicing. In summer 1963 this latter journey was timed to depart Kemble at 9.50 am after working the 9.33 from Cirencester Town. A third railbus would then work empty from Swindon to resume the Tetbury service which, being less frequent, had the necessary margin to achieve this changeover. The fourth vehicle remained at Swindon as a spare.* An additional duty of both these ECS trips was to call at Oaksey Halt to light the station lamps. It does not say much for the economics of the railbuses that a fleet of four trains was needed to keep one in service on each branch. Presumably all the diesel fitters at Swindon depot had to be trained in railbus maintenance even though these trains represented a small proportion of the motive power they serviced.

Opinions vary as to whether the original intention was to provide a through railbus service between Cirencester and Swindon. Lindsey Beard, then a BR management trainee based at Swindon, believes this to have been the case but that a decision was then taken before the railbuses commenced operation to ban them from carrying passengers on the main line in case the vehicles were too light to operate track circuits. (Similar doubts have been expressed about late 1980s rolling stock - in 1989 it appeared that new two-car 'Sprinter' diesel units might not always be activating track circuits between Kemble and Swindon.)

However, John Thomas believes there was no intention to run a Swindon passenger service with the railbuses. Given the inability of the A.C. Cars

* C.J. Leigh, 'The Railbus Experiment', *Railway World*, May 1978.

A view of a railbus at the buffer stops at Cirencester while to the right, mail bags can be seen on the platform and a Royal Mail van stands by.

Cotswold District Council

vehicles to couple with other rolling stock, it could be argued that a through Swindon service might well have led to serious overcrowding of a 46 seat vehicle, with one likely result being a restriction of the cheap fares which had been a major selling point for the new trains. Overcrowding did occur on Cirencester railbuses on market days and Saturdays; BR responded by increasing the service frequency in March 1959 and again in January 1960 but on both occasions this was to tap local demand for travel into Cirencester rather than farther afield.

It is highly likely that neither of the halts would have been built had direct trains between Cirencester Town and Swindon been a major feature of the new service. The additional stopping places, cheap fares and vigorous local publicity were an attempt to make the best of a service handicapped by a short-distance vehicle of low fuel capacity, low passenger capacity and not winning any prizes for the comfort of its ride. Recent experience on Regional Railways has suggested that passengers are prepared to pay rather more for services offering higher standards of comfort and convenience including more through journeys.

Nevertheless, the fact that the A.C. Cars railbuses had a top speed of 55 mph when the maximum permitted over both branches was 40 mph suggests that an element of main line running had been intended. Yet their 11-12 minute running time over the branch was not unattractive and is faster than the winter 1993/4 journey time over the Henley-on-Thames branch, which is of similar route mileage and also involves two intermediate stops.

Running railbuses from Cirencester Town did not noticeably extend the line's operating pattern. The branch continued to be worked by Electric Token and the speed limit was unchanged. The opening hours of Town signal box were not greatly altered from steam days. Thus in winter 1960/61 the weekday hours were from 6.40 am until the last train had been berthed; on Sundays the box was open from 5.45 pm to 12.20 am Monday morning. These Sunday hours represented no change on September 1951 when the weekday opening was 5.35 am to permit the passage of an early freight to Kemble.

Connections - the Achilles heel?

Although the railbuses gave the branch a more frequent service than it had enjoyed before, the answer to bus and car competition did not lie in new trains alone. The usefulness to through passengers of the more frequent service over the branch was diluted by the lack of a corresponding improvement to main line services at Kemble. There were actually fewer through passenger trains between Swindon and Gloucester in the early 1960s than nowadays. Hence the railbuses created few additional Cirencester/London connections. The services then operating on the main line were a mixed bag of Cheltenham-Paddington expresses, Swindon-Gloucester 'Cheltenham semi-fasts, Chalford-Gloucester auto-trains as well as short trips linking Swindon with Kemble or Purton; some in the last category did not even serve Kemble nor (with one Saturday evening exception) did any of the Chalford auto-trains. Today's roughly hourly weekday service between Swindon and Gloucester would have provided a much more regular series of connections with the railbus had the branch survived.

Without a comprehensive timetable revision in the Cotswolds, the experiment could not realise its potential. The absence of a Sunday train from Swindon serving Kemble between 3 pm and 8 pm meant that the first railbus trip up and down the branch did not connect with any down train. For most of this period there was no Swindon departure for Kemble between 5.48 pm and 8.17 pm on Mondays to Fridays. A missed opportunity in the 1961/62 winter timetable was the 7.55 pm (SX) Swindon-Minety which, had it been extended to Kemble, could have returned with a connection from the 8.20 Cirencester. So the latest departure from Cirencester Town to reach Swindon and London during the week was 7.35 pm, slightly improved to 7.50 pm in the final timetable.

The poor weekday evening service between Swindon and the Cirencester railbuses seems surprising in view of the rundown of the alternative M&SWJ route and its subsequent closure to passengers on 11th September, 1961. But by that time the future of rural branch lines generally was very uncertain, and any plans to increase their usefulness would have been in conflict with official thinking following the appointment of Dr Richard Beeching as BR Chairman that year.

The branch had provided almost the only rail link between Cirencester and Cheltenham or Gloucester after the slashing of services on the M&SWJ line on 30th June, 1958. In its last three years of passenger business, Watermoor station had just one northbound train Mondays to Fridays, allowing people about three hours in Cheltenham. By contrast there was a fair spread of services from Cirencester Town to north Gloucestershire via Kemble, although the branch had no train early enough to reach Gloucester or Cheltenham for normal office hours.

A Swindon-Hereford semi-fast provided a useful link for day trippers connecting from the first railbus which left Cirencester around 8 am. This same service got one to Stroud at 8.55 am but there was little choice of evening trains to suit returning workers; for instance, in summer 1963, one either got back to Cirencester at 5.17 pm or 7.26 pm. Nevertheless, the 5.17 arrival did suit students returning from Stroud Technical College whose train fares were paid for by the County Council.

The value of the railbuses for commuting was limited to Kemble and Park Leaze residents working normal office hours in Cirencester. Would-be commuters living off the branch tended to be served well in one direction but not the other, a situation due more to the lack of regular interval services on the main line than to any deficiencies in the branch timetable. So although the early morning Swindon-Hereford train enabled Purton and Minety people to catch the 8.30 am Kemble (due Cirencester 8.41), main line stopping trains were so irregular that the only feasible return service left Cirencester Town around 7 pm. Yet in steam days there had been a direct train from Cirencester Town (5.15 in 1952/3) serving all stations to Swindon.

John Thomas recalls that a reason local people often cited for not using the railbuses was the inconvenience of connections between the Cirencester and

Tetbury branches. While some inter-railbus connections were very good it was perhaps inevitable that when timetables were altered, connections between the two branches might suffer in order to maintain those with retimed main line trains.* This became more of a problem after the March 1962 economy cuts resulted in some lengthened waiting times at Kemble; the first morning train from Tetbury was a less attractive means of getting to Cirencester now that the wait at Kemble was slightly longer than the 24 minute trip from Tetbury itself. To have retimed the 8.30 am Kemble-Cirencester earlier would have broken the connection from Swindon although, as stated above, teatime services from Cirencester to stations between Kemble and Swindon were non-existent anyway.

The inclusion of Oaksey Halt, Minety, Purton and the Tetbury branch in the marketing of the Cirencester railbuses seems rather questionable, in view of the patchy connections between three separate local services. Such a marketing plan may well have begun life as a scheme for direct railbus services to Swindon. It would have been more sensible to have targeted the market for longer distance journeys from Cirencester, highlighting the best connections at Kemble.

Another unsatisfied demand was for through Cirencester-Tetbury trains but the track layout at Kemble made this impracticable; the Tetbury branch was only accessible from its bay platform and a through service would have needed three reversals.

Railbus No. W79977 is seen in the bay platform at Kemble after arrival with the 8.45 am from Cirencester. This service connected with the 'Cheltenham Spa Express', which can be seen in the background, headed on this occasion by 'Castle' class 4-6-0 No. 7000 *Viscount Portal*.   *P.J. Sharpe*

* For instance in winter 1961/2 the 2.05 pm Tetbury connected smartly into the 2.35 pm Kemble-Cirencester while for returning shoppers the 4.45 pm Cirencester had an eight minute connection at Kemble for Tetbury.

Railbus No. W79978 is seen as it leaves Cirencester with the 2 pm to Kemble on 5th August, 1963, August Bank Holiday. In the foreground is the pig dock while in the distance the engine shed can be seen.   *Michael Mensing*

Railbus No. W79978 is seen one mile south of Cirencester on the 2.20 pm from Kemble on 5th August, 1963.   *Michael Mensing*

Chapter Eight

A Climate for Closure

The train service economies of 5th March, 1962, applied all over the Western Region, cut the Saturday afternoon service over the branch back to hourly and upset some Cirencester/Tetbury connections. But the psychological effect of the cuts may have been greater since, after many years of stability and recently of growth in its train services, Cirencester now found itself with fewer trains. Coming six months after the closure of the M&SWJ line and Watermoor station to passengers, the reduction in services at Town seemed to be preparing Cirencester for a future in which railways would be very much in retreat.

While one arm of British Railways did its best to promote rail travel from stations such as Cirencester with regular adverts for cheap fares, opposing forces who saw little point in rural railways were gaining the ascendancy. Transport Minister Ernest Marples had appointed Dr Richard Beeching in 1961 to steer British Railways in a much more commercial direction. Even before the publication of his 'Reshaping' plan in March 1963, the ground was being prepared. Rural Councillors who went to see BR Management, in the hope of getting improved train services, were being told there was every likelihood of their local lines closing altogether.

The willingness that railway managers had shown in the 1950s to try their hand at experiments which might sustain branch lines was now giving way to mass elimination of activities deemed to be unprofitable. The change of official direction was driven largely by the appointment of senior managers from private industry - in many cases people whose heart was not in railways - but this itself reflected a changed political atmosphere; rising car ownership was producing a less public transport-conscious nation. Once a consensus had developed in which people were expecting progressively less of their rail and bus services, the Beeching proposals were assured their passage.

With hindsight, neither a policy of closing branch lines nor of tinkering piecemeal with railbuses and new halts really addressed the problem of how the railways could meet the challenge of an increasingly motorised society. Main line services should have been revitalised before the fine details of improvements to branch lines were worked out. Had Swindon-Gloucester services been recast on a regular interval basis first, the investment in the Cirencester branch would have rested on a firmer base.

It was easier for a programme of rail closures to get off the ground in 1963 because the roads were less crowded and bus services more extensive than today. The few rail closure proposals of the 1980s tended to meet highly professional opposition and much scrutiny in the media. Perhaps people have become less credulous of officialdom as so many public utilities have been sacrificed on the altar of economy in the past 30 years, particularly in rural areas.

But in 1963 sweeping generalisations about railways being a drain on the taxpayer were politically respectable, perhaps for the very reason that many train services had been out of touch with what the consumer wanted. In July of

Two views of '16XX' class 0-6-0PT No. 1664 with a goods train at Cirencester in August 1963. In the view above the signal box and cattle dock can be clearly seen.   *(Both) Paul Strong*

that year, at a public meeting in Cirencester's Corn Hall, local MP Nicholas Ridley was reported as describing BR's deficits as a misuse of public money that might be diverted to education, health, roads and building. His thinking may well have been influenced by other rail closures in his constituency, namely the M&SWJ line in 1961 and the Fairford and Cheltenham-Kingham branches in 1962. He claimed, 'Three branch lines had closed in the area recently and there had been little inconvenience caused . . . What we have got to ask ourselves is whether it is fair to use public money on ourselves when it might be spent on something else'.*

He made no mention of how the three lines might have been seen off by unsatisfactory services, particularly after the 1958 timetable cuts. Perhaps this was because he had only represented the area since October 1959. He expressed his conviction that the solution to the closure proposal lay in better bus services; if people would tell him what improvements were required to replace the railway, he would do his best to see they were introduced.

Disputed arithmetic

Formal closure proposals for the Cirencester and Tetbury branches had been published in mid-June 1963, less than three months after the Beeching Report itself. The losses allegedly incurred by the two routes were a drop in the ocean compared with BR's national deficit, so the almost indecent haste to close them suggests either that closure had been under serious consideration for some time previously or that lopping the two branches was the prelude to rumoured plans to eliminate the Swindon-Gloucester main line. John Thomas believes that Management's intentions did indeed go further than the published proposals to close the branches and also most stations on the main line.

Local suspicions of sinister plans to divert Paddington-Cheltenham expresses via Badminton and Westerleigh Junction may have been fuelled by the apparent unwillingness of BR's Bristol divisional management to offer a reasoned argument why closure was necessary. When representatives of Cirencester Urban District Council met the divisional marketing & sales manager on 23rd August and asked whether it was not possible to operate the branch at a profit he allegedly said 'I can definitely say this scheme must go forward'.†

Such an evasive reply might equally have concealed intentions to redevelop the Town station site, another suspicion in objectors' minds. Or it may have been policy to close lines first which had been showpieces of recent experiments to attract traffic lest anyone should find living contradiction of the new orthodoxy.

The statutory notice for the closure proposal outlined an amended Cirencester-Kemble-Tetbury bus service but the frequency compared very unfavourably with that of the trains. Just four journeys from Cirencester were envisaged on Mondays to Fridays; the first departure at 6.56 am from outside Town station would not even serve Kemble station and was essentially to get a bus to Tetbury in time to pick up commuters. Last buses were scheduled to leave Cirencester at 4.35 pm four hours earlier than the latest train, and from Kemble at 6.12 pm, compared with a latest train departure of 8.55 pm. While

* *Wilts & Gloucestershire Standard*, 26.7.63.
† *Wilts & Gloucestershire Standard*, 21.9.63.

the Saturday timetable would be less pathetic involving eight journeys each way, access between Cirencester and the main line system would still be severely limited.

For instance the final departure from Paddington reaching Kemble in time for an onward bus connection would be 1.55 pm; even this would involve a 45-minute wait at Swindon for a train to Kemble, where an incredible 81 minutes would elapse whilst the bus travelled to Tetbury and back before proceeding to Cirencester. The train service which BR was trying to close allowed people to leave Paddington as late as 7 pm (SX) and 8 pm (SO).

A shoestring bus service may have been theoretically profitable assuming people would use it but its publication may have served to divert objections from the principle of closing the railway and to redefine the issue in people's minds as one of whether proposed buses were adequate. But the inconvenient questions about whether the line could not be run more economically refused to go away. That very July the National Council on Inland Transport (NCIT) published its appraisal of the line's costs, claiming that there were currently 30 season ticket holders and quoting an average of 80 passengers apiece on two morning and evening trains for a recent Saturday.* Given that the railbus had a nominal seating capacity of 46 and floorspace to allow perhaps 20 people to stand in tolerable comfort, this was a remarkable level of overcrowding. NCIT also quoted 3,000 tickets to London being sold from Cirencester over the previous 12 months.

Their report based the weekly running costs of the Cirencester railbus on a mileage of 807, which included the daily empty trips between Kemble and Swindon for servicing. This was said to require 112 gallons of diesel fuel at 2s. 6d. per gallon, i.e. £14 per week, plus traincrew costs of £60 per week for two drivers and two guards paid £15 each. This seems a shade too amateurish as drivers were better paid than guards and the rates quoted were on the low side if overtime, Sunday payments and relief staff were taken into account. Moreover, the costs of maintaining the vehicles at Swindon needed to enter the equation, as did utilities such as gas, water and electricity, not only at Town station but also at Swindon Motive Power Depot. Yet even though NCIT's estimate of £74 per week (£3,850 per year) to run the passenger service was almost certainly too low, it was difficult to see how BR could arrive at an annual deficit of £7,800 for the branch after including revenue.

The arguments seemed to revolve around the staff numbers needed to run the passenger service. Both sides may have utilised unrealistic figures. NCIT, which claimed that BR had based its closure arithmetic on a staff of 40 for the Cirencester branch, said the actual number of employees was 19, with scope for a further reduction and £30 weekly saving if Town signal box were to be closed. But BR Management was not interested in spending money to simplify the signalling of a line it wished to close.

Many of the 15 employees over and above the four needed to crew the railbuses would only be surplus if the branch were also to lose its freight service. Naturally, total closure would enable expenditure to be avoided on track or other structures but it was disingenuous of BR to claim that withdrawing the passenger trains would by itself produce such large savings.

* *Wilts & Gloucestershire Standard*, 2.8.63.

Battle is joined

The public hearing to consider objections into the closure proposal for both branches from Kemble was held at St Peter's Hall, Cirencester on 13th September, 1963, conducted by the South Western Area Transport Users Consultative Committee (TUCC), the statutory body required by law to report to the Minister of Transport on the level of hardship likely to arise from rail closures. Any decision to authorise or refuse closure rested with the Minister; prior to the 1962 Transport Act the regional TUCCs could make such decisions themselves, although they could be over-ruled by the (generally pro-closure) Central TUCC in London.

This transfer of power away from TUCCs was emphasised by the South Western Chairman, Major-General W.E.V. Abraham, to the 30 or so participants when he opened the enquiry. Pointing out that his Committee could only report on expected hardship to passengers and how it might be relieved, he added that the TUCC had not been able to define precisely what hardship amounted to. (The definition remains elusive today, as demonstrated by the Settle-Carlisle closure battle in the 1980s.)

A central theme in the objections was that projected bus services could not handle existing rail traffic which, from BR's own census taken in January, amounted to over 2,000 passengers per week on the Cirencester branch. It was not only the scarcity of proposed buses that drew objectors' fire; they were claimed to be less suitable for prams and heavy luggage.

These points were made by Anthony Quick, Headmaster of Rendcomb College, who spoke of the difficulty of conveying his scholars' suitcases by bus. He argued that parents might be dissuaded from selecting his school if Cirencester were to lose its 'easily accessible station'. The effect on the local economy was also stressed by Ewen housewife Vera Pope, a regular user of Park Leaze Halt, who argued the need for good public transport to attract and retain domestic staff.

Mr Quick lashed the proposed service of four buses a day from Cirencester to Kemble; this would virtually isolate the town from London unless people were prepared to contemplate BR's suggestion of travelling by bus to Swindon, a journey of an hour. This he regarded as a dark hint of future plans to close the Swindon-Gloucester line.

Mrs Pope, who had recently organised a demonstration of pram-wheeling mothers in an attempt to impress Nicholas Ridley of the need for rail transport, said buses would be near useless to Ewen in winter because its access to the main road was a path which tended to get bogged down, as had happened earlier that year. Were residents expected to hibernate, she asked?

She also told of how she had arranged for a family group with a pushchair to travel into Cirencester by train and by bus. This exercise had been to point out the additional financial burden that closure would place on families without cars because Bristol Omnibus fares were higher than rail for children and day return journeys. Waiting for connections between main line trains and infrequent buses at Kemble would also make hospital visiting more difficult.

The effect of closure on the town's traffic problems was also raised at the

Cirencester station viewed from near the cattle dock; railbus No. W79975 is at the buffer stops, 19th August, 1963.   *Roger Joanes*

Kemble with a railbus at the bay platform viewed from the Cirencester end. In the distance a 'Hymek' can be seen on an up main line passenger train.   *Andrew Muckley*

hearing. Mr B. Elliott representing Cirencester Rural District Council claimed that in summer buses took three times longer between Cirencester and Kemble because of congestion in the town. He also described the road to Kemble as hazardous with a notable blackspot at the Kemble turn from the Cirencester-Tetbury road. (Did many people appreciate the irony of the local paper's use of adjacent columns for the announcement of the venue for the rail closure hearing and its report of a young woman's death in a car crash on the Kemble road?)*

Several objectors undermined the credibility of British Railways' argument that closure would save public money. C.R. Mullings on behalf of Cirencester Urban District Council disclosed that the UDC had learned only the previous day that closing the line would incur the Post Office an additional £750 per year for collecting mail at Kemble station. Derek Leigh for Gloucestershire County Council revealed that additional buses for students attending Stroud Technical College would cost ratepayers an extra £1,000 annually. Mr Mullings also said BR had admitted that a more generous frequency of buses would require a subsidy. So where was the saving in closing the line?

British Railways was represented at the hearing by Mr N.S. Taylor, divisional marketing & sales manager, whom UDC representatives had met in Bristol a few weeks previously to plead for the line. Mr Mullings now told the inquiry that in May his Council had been quoted a figure of £12,700 by BR as the annual loss on the Cirencester Town branch but by June the deficit had been revised to £7,800. Mr Taylor now confirmed what he had advised the UDC in August, i.e. that the higher amount took account of longer term plans to remove the line's freight services as well.

Mr Mullings rounded on the inadequacy of BR's financial case which he said was based on unsubstantiated figures, in sharp contrast to the UDC's own audited accounts which were required to be available for public inspection. Too much had been left out of the calculations for the Urban Council to be convinced that closure would bring a net saving to the community. As for the intention to withdraw freight services from Cirencester Town, this abandonment of the branch would represent a destruction of the taxpayer's capital.

Essentially, the local authorities were challenging the logic of replacing a multi-purpose rail service conveying workers, scholars, shoppers, parcels and mails, by separate specialist road vehicles. BR's reply to the question of school transport was that the responsibility lay with local authorities, in the case of state schools, and with parents, in the case of private schools like Rendcomb College.

The positions of the opposing camps could be summarised thus: On the one hand British Railways wished to divest itself of traditional social obligations, in order to better its own profit and loss account, thereby (so it claimed) saving taxpayers' money. From the opposite viewpoint, Cirencester and district stood to gain nothing but inferior public transport, reduced accessibility and higher rates if the line were closed.

The Rendcomb Headmaster argued that public transport was in danger of serious decline because the Railways Board took too insular a view of its obligations: 'The railways have been so busy cultivating their particular

---

* *Wilts & Gloucestershire Standard*, 2.3.63.

cabbage patch, the railway accounts, that they have forgotten some very important figures'.

He explained the anticipated increase in the UK population and the pressures this would create on space. Railways, he said, were easily the most economic transport system in terms of space consumed; was it possible to believe that the answer lay in dismantling the public transport system and putting the maximum number of cars on the roads? 'Instead of working out a sensible national system and then making the books balance, they are breaking up the transport system to balance the books'.*

But neither Mr Quick's long-term perspective, nor the numerous other grounds of objection, appear to have made much impression on the TUCC, who were later reported as having recommended additional buses to relieve the hardship expected from the rail closure.†

The war of words continued for several months after the official hearing. Lord Stonham, representing the National Council on Inland Transport, said Cirencester Town station did in fact produce a healthy profit, citing annual revenue of £30,820 against operating costs of £11,000. Nicholas Ridley responded that the revenue figure quoted by Lord Stonham had included the complete fares for tickets sold to destinations beyond Kemble as well as local journeys on the branch; misleading statements made it even harder for people to accept closure 'when it is without doubt a necessity'.#

Anthony Quick retaliated by attacking 'the Beeching accountancy' for only crediting the line with revenue equivalent to journeys between Cirencester and Kemble; in the real world, the probable loss of revenue after closure would be much greater. Several of his pupils had made known their intentions to travel from home by car throughout rather than pay taxi fares from Kemble to Rendcomb.

Even if the line were truly loss-making, he said, a civilised society required public transport, particularly for the young, old or infirm. Denouncing the Beeching closure programme as 'assuming that the new affluence of society should be used to discriminate against the worst off', he condemned it as 'one of the most selfish proposals in years'.

The principal objectors seem to have become disenchanted with the TUCC hearing as an effective means of protest. The two Cirencester Councils made further representations to the Minister in the hope of saving the line. Vera Pope was reported as saying that, although Major-General Abrahams had allowed her a fair hearing, she felt the exercise had been a waste of time. Mr Quick blamed the 1962 Transport Act for excluding possible economies in operation from the scope of what TUCCs could recommend to the Minister. More recently, David Henshaw has concluded, in his study of the political background to the closure programme, that TUCCs were reluctant to adopt arguments which could be construed as accusing the Railways Board of false accounting.§

---

* *Wilts & Gloucestershire Standard*, 20.9.63.
† *Wilts & Gloucestershire Standard*, 15.11.63.
# *Wilts & Gloucestershire Standard*, 25.10.63.
§ D. Henshaw, *The Great Railway Conspiracy*, Leading Edge, 1991.

At the eleventh hour the protesters gained a degree of support from Nicholas Ridley, hitherto unconvinced of the need for a railway at Cirencester. On 30th December he wrote to Ernest Marples, thanking the Minister for granting him an interview and referring to local concern about the railway. There would, he said, definitely be hardship if people had to rely on existing bus services. Asking the Minister to examine the financial case before reaching a decision, he said: 'People feel that the figures given by the Board are false and do not show the true financial position'.

He argued that unless the Minister could demonstrate that the financial position was as stated, and the hardship factor could be resolved, this closure should not be agreed to.*

Ex-LMS Stanier class '5' 4-6-0 No. 44966 is seen on a freight train on 7th March, 1964. It was unusual motive power on the Gloucester-Swindon route. The Cirencester branch sweeps away to the right. Note the BR station sign for Kemble which reads 'Change for Cirencester and Tetbury'.   *Hugh Ballantyne*

* *Wilts & Gloucestershire Standard, 17.1.64.*

'14XX' class 0-4-2T No. 1472 propels Gloucestershire Railway Society special from Kemble and approaches Somerford Road bridge on 5th April, 1964.   *David Lawrence*

No. 1472 Kemble with the Gloucestershire Railway Society special train on 5th April, 1964.
R.W. Hinton Collection

Chapter Nine

Killed by Marples

The text of Mr Ridley's letter and the Ministerial reply to it were released with the press announcement of Mr Marples' consent to the closure proposal. In a letter to British Railways dated 13th January, 1964 the Minister said he accepted the TUCC's recommendation of additional bus services to relieve hardship likely to arise from closing the line. His reply to Mr. Ridley's letter asserted that the financial data supplied to the public hearing, i.e. an annual expenditure of £11,000 against revenue of £3,500, represented the direct costs and income attributable to the passenger service. Marples described this type of statistic as the most suitable for the purpose of TUCC hearings. Possibly he was aware that further details such as the portion of ticket sales for journeys beyond Kemble might confirm objectors' impressions that closing the branch would lose BR more money through loss of long distance business than would allegedly be saved by the closure. Short branch lines from sizeable towns to a main line junction were badly penalised by this distorted accounting which ignored the revenue fed to the rest of the rail network. Very few lines of this type survived a closure proposal.

Ernest Marples also claimed that the £7,500 annual loss quoted for the line had if anything understated the savings to be realised from closure.* While a truer assessment of the line's costs would need to include the maintenance and likely renewals of bridges and permanent way, the financial picture could still be coloured by whether these civil engineering costs were based on an average for the BR network or whether they were a reasonable forecast for maintaining a particular stretch of railway over a specified period.

Whether the line was presented as being financially healthy or as a terminal case might also have depended on how its capital assets - stations, structures and rolling stock - were accounted for. Passenger rolling stock on BR was normally depreciated over 25 years, so that many of the older trains in use today have a capital asset value of zero. By contrast the railbuses were almost new when introduced on the Cirencester and Tetbury branches and five years old when passenger services ceased. It is possible that when BR decided to propose closure of the railbus services the capital cost of the vehicles (which had no place in Beeching's vision of the future anyway) was then written off over a much shorter working life so as to claim greater savings from closure.

The axe is poised

Even during the previous summer, when the closure proposal was hot news, cheap train fares from Cirencester had appeared in the local press with the slogan 'Travel Western to avoid congestion'. Possibly BR had placed a contract for advertising space some time before the Beeching hit-list had been finalised;

* *Wilts & Gloucestershire Standard*, 17.1.64.

or perhaps there were people in its Bristol Divisional Office who had more faith in their branch lines than had the senior Management.

The latter theory might explain a remarkable piece of timing on BR's part. Just as it formally announced that the railbus services would cease from 6th April, 1964, came the news that Cirencester would enjoy an additional train from 27th January. This commendable attempt to attract more passengers had no doubt been formulated before the Minister's decision was known and involved retiming the first weekday railbus to leave Cirencester 20 minutes earlier at 7.35 am so as to preserve its connection into the 7.05 am Cheltenham-Swindon, which now ran 10 minutes earlier. The earlier arrival in Kemble of the railbus at 7.47 am, nearly 45 minutes before its next working back with commuters, allowed an extra trip to be fitted in leaving Kemble at 7.52 am and returning from Cirencester at 8.08.

Reactions to the Minister's verdict included a feeling of disillusionment with the decision-making processes. Vera Pope said the latest topic of discussion in the railbuses was of where to shop instead of Cirencester. Rather than use buses which were not convenient for prams, shoppers were planning to go by train from Kemble to Swindon or Stroud where lower prices would reclaim the higher rail fare. She also accused Cirencester businessmen of being too apathetic about the rail closure.* Possibly they were pinning their faith on more parking spaces to increase trade as contemporary town planning tended to assume universal car ownership was not far off.

The closure announcement also prompted people who had hitherto been silent to make their views public. Some lucid criticism was made by John Bowyer, a London barrister who was Labour Parliamentary candidate for Cirencester & Tewkesbury. He argued that the Government was treating railway finances in isolation from the true costs of increased road transport. He also claimed that the line's cash takings were six to eight times the £3,500 quoted as the annual income of the branch.

Mr Bowyer added that a Labour Government would draw up a plan for all forms of transport and he would be very surprised if such a study did not reprieve the Cirencester branch. Nicholas Ridley retorted that a Labour administration would not have acted differently from the Conservatives on the issue of rail closures.† And he was to be proved right in so far as the Wilson Government elected later that year was to continue the mass extermination of rural railways. Both Governments seem to have regarded the Mid-West of England as a soft target for rail cuts, not least in Gloucestershire where almost every proposed closure received Ministerial approval.

Last Rites

Vera Pope, the tireless campaigner who had been reportedly banned for life from the House of Commons after scattering anti-closure leaflets from the Visitors' Gallery the previous November, sent out black-edged invitations for a beer and sherry 'Bereavement Party' to take place at Town station on the last night of passenger operations, Sunday 5th April. Among those invited were

---

* *Wilts & Gloucestershire Standard*, 24.1.64.
† *Wilts & Gloucestershire Standard*, 31.1.64 and 21.2.64.

Ernest Marples, Nicholas Ridley and General Sir Brian Robertson who had been BR Chairman at the time the railbuses came into service and who lived locally. Mrs Pope advised the press that the party would begin aboard the 8.35 pm from Kemble which would convey an effigy of the Transport Minister for ceremonial burning at midnight.*

A more traditional railway funeral was arranged by Gloucestershire Railway Society in the form of a two-coach special train hauled by 0-4-2T No. 1472 of Gloucester Horton Road shed. The special, which carried 80 enthusiasts at a fare of 25s. from Gloucester, also traversed the Tetbury branch and reached Cirencester at 4.30 pm. Normal passenger services, commencing with the 6.15 pm Cirencester, were worked by railbus, No. W79977.

At the appointed hour Mrs Pope tried to light the effigy of the Minister who had overruled more polite forms of protest, but she was restrained by two railway policemen warning of the proximity of a gas main. They ordered her to take the dummy off the station premises. Their alertness may even have prevented a railway tragedy from becoming a human one as well. So the Transport Minister's image was set ablaze on the pavement of the main Bristol road outside the station forecourt as people spilled into the street to watch. A policeman tried to beat out the flames but this only made 'Ernest Marples' burn more vigorously for a while. 'Hundreds jeered when the effigy was burned' recalled the *Wilts & Gloucestershire Standard* which noted that the police took Mrs Pope's name and address. This was not to be the only insult hurled that night at the man who had signed away Cirencester's train services (and over 120 years of history), for the last passenger train from Town station at 11.30 pm, driven by George Williams, had carried a wreath inscribed 'Killed by Marples'.†

The Tetbury branch closed completely that same weekend and its funeral on Saturday 4th April had been equally colourful though less bitter. A coffin of empty whisky bottles was carried aboard the final Tetbury railbus for transfer into a London train at Kemble, addressed to Dr Beeching. Leading the procession in a dark veil was Janet Peare, daughter of the licensee of the Trouble House Inn and a commuter to Stroud Technical College. There had been much less opposition to the Tetbury closure - in fact Tetbury RDC's spokesman had told the TUCC's hearing that all it was asking for were several extra buses. Now the RDC complained that buses required as a condition of the Minister's approval of closure were inadequate. Hence the poem attached to the coffin highlighted the predicament of travellers like Janet Peare: 'She will miss the friendly hooter and have to buy a scooter'.

Rumours soon circulated that the Cirencester Town station site had been sold for redevelopment. John Bowyer, who attended the 'bereavement party' before returning to London via the final passenger train, now claimed that a land sale was almost clinched and would involve the main station buildings but not the goods yard. His election agent, Mary Fitzgerald, was reported as having witnessed his hearing of the deal from a reliable source.

British Railways denied that any sale had taken place but admitted they would consider offers. The rumours may have arisen from confusion with plans to convert part of the ex-M&SWJ line, newly disused with the ending of freight services at Watermoor on 1st April, into a bypass road.#

---

* *Wilts & Gloucestershire Standard*, 3.4.64.

† *Wilts & Gloucestershire Standard*, 11.4.64.

Wilts & Gloucestershire Standard, 3 4.64.

Left: The station building at Cirencester in spring 1973, just prior to the removal of the platform canopy.
D.J. Viner/Corinium Museum/Cotswold District Council

Below: Cirencester station building from the Kemble end in May 1990.
Ross Grover

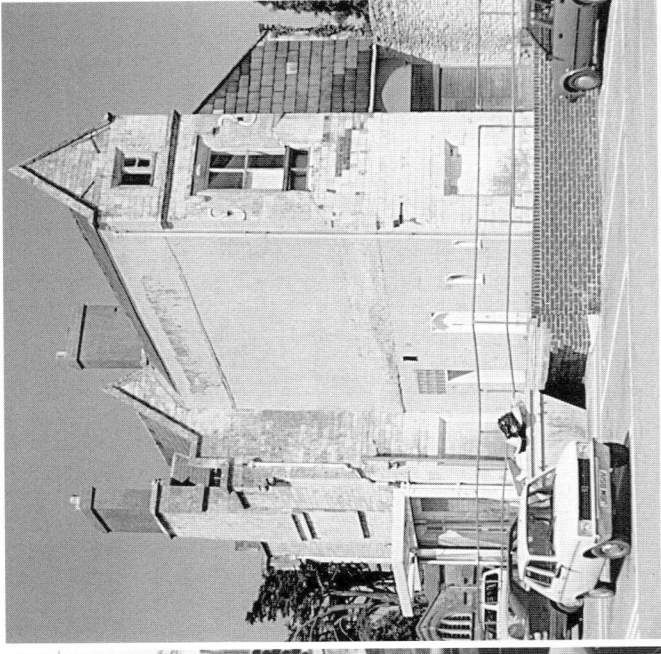

Experience elsewhere suggests that disposal of Town station may have been under discussion by the time of the Minister's decision, if not before. Other centrally sited stations such as Cheltenham St James and Yeovil Town were closed in the mid-1960s, later to become car parks. More recently, the hasty disposal of the Tunbridge Wells West station site after its closure in 1985 points to the property deal, rather than any operating losses, as being the motive behind closure.

The railbuses were stored at Swindon for a few months before being redeployed further west. BR's Plymouth divisional management, perhaps less enthusiastic for the policy of 'closures than their colleagues at Bristol, were revising services between Bodmin, Wadebridge and Padstow to incorporate a railbus shuttle between Bodmin North and a new halt at Boscarne where passengers could connect with Bodmin Road-Padstow trains. Two of the A.C. Cars railbuses went to Cornwall in the summer of 1964 until both passenger services ended on 30th January, 1967. Meanwhile the two sister vehicles had been operating the service between Yeovil Town and Pen Mill stations which lasted until 3rd October, 1966. Railbuses Nos. W79976 and W79978 were transferred to Scotland early in 1967, being withdrawn in February 1968 with the ending of railbus operation on BR. Both have been preserved. No. W79976 was for many years a static exhibit at the Somerset Railway Museum, Bleadon, later moving to the Bodmin & Wenford Railway and then for a brief spell on the Mid-Norfolk Railway before joining No. W79978 on the Colne Valley Railway. No. W79978 had resided in working order on the North Yorkshire Moors Railway in the 1970s.

Final curtain at Cirencester

After the Minister's decision on the passenger service was announced, an interim arrangement was made to convey parcels traffic in a van attached to the early morning freight train down the branch. Before returning from Cirencester with the up freight, the locomotive was to run light to Kemble to collect a second van which would work back with parcels forwarded from Cirencester. This was a short term measure pending the concentration of Cirencester's freight at Swindon (see *Appendix Five*).

The branch remained open for freight but on 14th June, 1964 all tracks in the passenger station including the lead into the engine shed (disused since passenger services ended) were taken out of use. Town signal box was closed from this date, as was the ground frame opposite the pig dock at the station throat.* The branch was now worked on a 'one engine in steam' basis and the only run-round facility was now through the Kemble end of the goods yard. From 15th June the service was confined to Coal Class traffic.

The branch received its last consignment of timber in the spring of 1964. Reg Cleveland, who worked for builders' merchants A. Harman & Son, has recalled unloading some 80 wagons over a three-week period at night because the firm was busy serving customers in the daytime.†

---

* R.A. Cooke, *Track Layout Diagrams*, Section 20.
† Cirencester Chamber of Commerce News, 25.11.87.

Kemble station viewed from the Swindon end in May 1990. The remaining short section of the Cirencester branch can be seen on the right.   *Ross Grover*

The end of the line. The remains of the Cirencester branch in May 1990.   *Ross Grover*

During the winter of 1964/65 a Class 9 freight train from Swindon to Cirencester was scheduled to run Mondays, Wednesdays and Fridays only, powered by a '16XX' 0-6-0 pannier tank. The Swindon crew were rostered from 5.05 am to 1.05 pm and the trip had the following schedule:

		am			am
Swindon shed (Light Engine)	dep.	5.50			
Swindon Transfer Yard	arr.	6.00		dep.	6.05
Kemble	arr.	6.50	Shunt	dep.	7.20
Cirencester Town	arr.	7.33	Shunt	dep.	8.30
Kemble	arr.	8.43			
Kemble	Light Engine			dep.	9.15
Swindon shed	arr.	9.43			

Sometimes 204 hp 0-6-0 diesel shunters were used instead of a steam locomotive. The limited shunting time allowance at Cirencester reflected the reduction in freight facilities offered from 15th June. Perhaps this explains the lack of local press coverage for the ending of all freight services and complete closure of the branch on 4th October, 1965. The line had latterly been operational for a couple of hours each week to service the local coal merchant. Public interest in the line may well have evaporated once it became clear that the incoming Labour Government was not going to reverse any of Ernest Marples' closure decisions. So much for the generous coverage in the local newspaper of the railbuses, excursion fares and the fight to keep the line open. Perhaps the very excitement which attended the last day of passenger services had convinced locals and enthusiasts alike that the line had already passed into history. There was in any case no shortage of railway closures, many of them equally contentious, in Mid-Western England in the mid-1960s.

Track lifting took place in 1966 except for a short stub at Kemble reaching 91 m. 10 ch., retained as an engineers' siding. This in turn was cut back to the end of the bay platform in about 1986 to provide more parking space at the station. During the 1990s the bay, which has long lost its platform canopy, has stabled Civil Engineering department wagons from time to time.

The site of the engine shed at Cirencester, showing the wheelstops and inspection pit in 1973.
D.J. Viner/Corinium Museum/Cotswold District Council

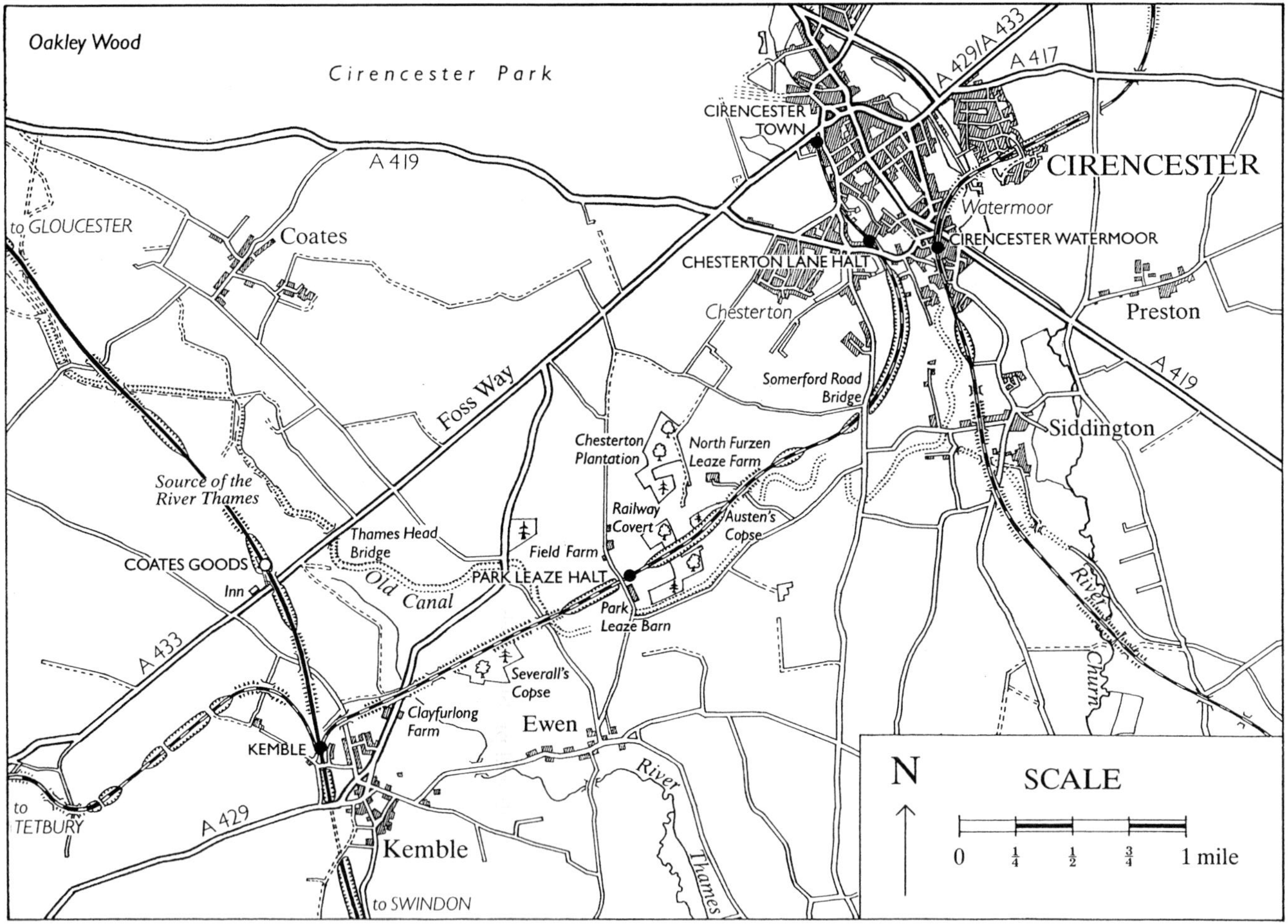
Oakley Wood
Cirencester Park
A 419
to GLOUCESTER
Coates
CIRENCESTER TOWN
CIRENCESTER
A 429/A 433
A 417
Watermoor
CIRENCESTER WATERMOOR
CHESTERTON LANE HALT
Chesterton
Preston
A 419
Somerford Road Bridge
Siddington
Foss Way
Chesterton Plantation
North Furzen Leaze Farm
Source of the River Thames
Railway Covert
Austen's Copse
Thames Head Bridge
Field Farm
COATES GOODS
PARK LEAZE HALT
Inn
Old Canal
Park Leaze Barn
River Churn
A 433
Severall's Copse
Clayfurlong Farm
Ewen
KEMBLE
to TETBURY
A 429
River Thames
Kemble
to SWINDON
N
SCALE
0 ¼ ½ ¾ 1 mile

Chapter Ten

The Line Described

Kemble to Chesterton Lane

The Cirencester branch rails diverged from those of the Swindon-Gloucester main line at Kemble East Ground Frame, now simply known as Kemble Ground Frame and situated 90 miles 73 chains from Paddington. This junction was by the station side of the overbridge at the Swindon end of the station.

The original 1836 C&GWUR Bill had proposed a triangular layout at Kemble. Even after this feature was dropped, the logical position for Kemble station, once the Gordon family could be persuaded to accept a public station on their estate, was in the fork of the Cirencester and Gloucester lines since this was a spacious site providing for public access to the platforms at ground level. By contrast, a site east of the junction would have been constricted by the deep cutting approaching Kemble tunnel. Thus it was more probably the limitations of the Kemble site, rather than the earlier opening of the line to Cirencester than that to Gloucester, which resulted in the sharply curved bay for branch trains and the triangular arrangement of station buildings between the branch and up main platform faces. Still to be seen in the apex of this platform are attractive gardens between what was the Cirencester bay and the cloistered walkway leading from the ticket office to the main line platforms. Intending passengers could reach the branch platform either through the booking hall or directly from the station forecourt through a pair of ornate wooden doors in the outer wall, close to the present bus stop.

Pleasing though this layout may have been to the eye, it was to present operational problems when the East and West signal boxes at either end of the main line platforms were replaced by one prefabricated box next to the water tower at the Gloucester end of the down platform in 1929. This made it inconvenient for the Kemble signalman to deliver and retrieve the electric staff for the branch train. So a small wooden cabin with a slate roof was provided on the bay platform, housing a 10-lever ground frame and the electric staff instrument. The new ground frame also operated points at the Cirencester end of the bay as these were not visible from the new signal box.*

A runround and small yard opposite the bay line allowed for a certain amount of shunting. Beyond the end of the platform were sidings, serving the Permanent Way Department, on the down side. These sidings were flanked by packers' huts, stores and the office of the Kemble P.W. Inspector, whose residence was the imposing detached house which still overlooks the station forecourt today. Kemble had a small goods yard alongside the Tetbury bay which dealt with covered vans but most freight for the locality was dealt with at Coates goods station, a mile north of Kemble on the Gloucester line and close to the Thames Head Inn. Coates (known as Tetbury Road until 1908) closed on 1st July, 1963, having ceased to be a passenger station on 1st May, 1882, when the present Kemble station buildings were opened.

* A. Vaughan, *GWR Junction Stations*, Ian Allan, 1988.

The main line platforms of Kemble station looking towards Swindon on 8th August, 1934.
Mowat Collection/W.R. Burton

A view of the Cirencester bay platform and run-round loops from the junction end, with a carriage in P.W. sidings in the distance, 8th September, 1953.   *Rokeby Collection*

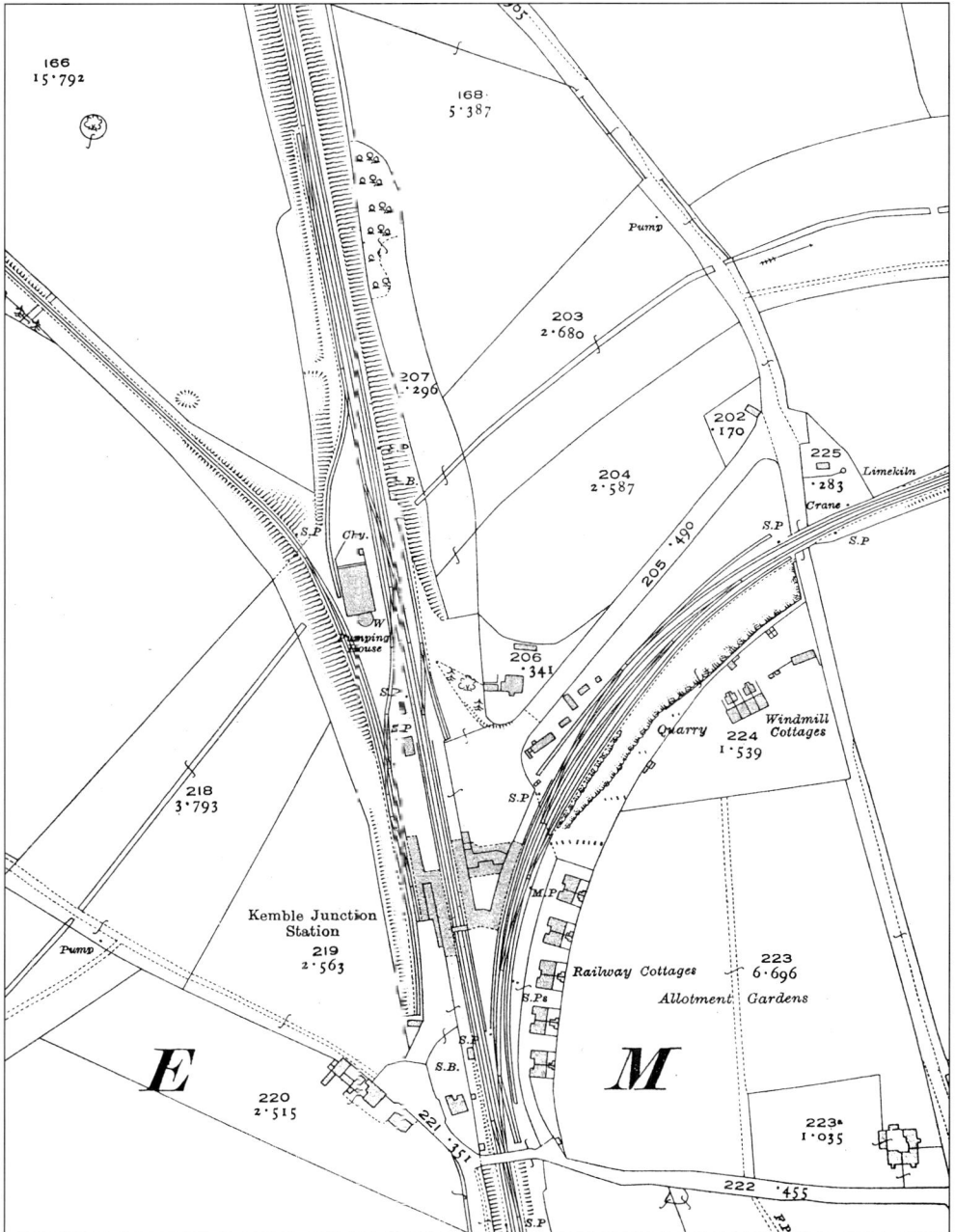

166
15·792

168
5·387

Pump

203
2·680

207
·296

202
·170

225
·283

Limekiln

Crane

204
2·587

205 ·490

S.P

S.P

S.P

Chy.

Pumping House

W

206
·341

Windmill Cottages
224
1·539

Quarry

S.P

218
3·793

S.P

Kemble Junction
Station
219
2·563

M.P.

223
6·696

Railway Cottages

S.Ps

Allotment Gardens

Pump

E

M

S.P.

S.B.

223·
1·035

220
2·515

221 ·551

222 ·455

S.P

Kemble Junction station. The branch to the left is for Tetbury, while the line to the right is for Cirencester. *Reproduced from the 25", 1921 Ordnance Survey Map*

The very basic Park Leaze Halt looking towards Cirencester.   *Lens of Sutton*

Park Leaze Halt looking towards Kemble. The notice board shows the name of the halt.
                                                                               Lens of Sutton

The branch curved north-eastwards away from the station area to cross over an unclassified road connecting Kemble village with the A433 Foss Way. This bridge survived until the mid-1980s when the station car park was enlarged over the site of the coal yard. The yard had been used by local coal merchants Cyril Austin and George Mills whose lorries had entered it from this road. As late as 1987 some rusty palings were evidence that the yard had existed.

Since leaving Kemble the line had begun a gentle climb of 1 in 330 which continued for about seven-eighths of a mile. After passing some quarries on the up side, the line now climbed an embankment to cross over not only the A429 Cirencester-Malmesbury road but also the infant River Thames about ½ mile from Kemble, just north of Clayfurlong Farm. This three-arch stone bridge, now demolished, was about 1 mile from Thames Head and was the most upstream bridge of that river by road or railway.

The line remained on an embankment and continued almost dead straight for about nine-tenths of a mile, passing Severalls Copse before making yet another simultaneous crossing of road and waterway at Ewen Wharf. Here the line went over the Thames & Severn Canal (abandoned between 1927 and 1933 by the GWR who had bought it up in 1882) just before the waterway ran alongside a minor road from Ewen village to the A429.

Soon afterwards the line dropped into a shallow cutting for about 1 mile to reach **Park Leaze Halt**, (92 m. 42 ch.), opened on 4th January, 1960. It was sited on the Cirencester side of a bridge carrying a lane off the Ewen-Siddington road. This is now the last surviving overbridge on the route. The halt amounted to a short sleeper-built platform at rail height on the down side of the line. It served Ewen village about a mile to the south but more immediately several farms. Public access was via a sloping path, now heavily overgrown, although still traceable at the time of my last visit in 1995 when the platform site was marked by a clump of undergrowth.

Park Leaze bridge was of stone construction but with a layer of brick underneath the arch. By 1987 it had become much overgrown by ivy. John Nicholas has suggested that the continued existence of the bridge may be due to its proximity to a water main. A more curious survival at the site are lengths of broad gauge bridge rail used as end fence posts near what was the entrance to the platform.

The halt probably served some 20 people directly but was useful to Ewen villagers who needed to visit Cirencester. It was less attractive for journeys between Ewen, Kemble and beyond since the walk from Ewen to Kemble was only slightly longer than that from Ewen to the halt itself.

Park Leaze must rank as one of the shortest-lived stations in postwar Britain, being in use for four and a quarter years. But 30 years were to pass after its closure before another new station was opened within Gloucestershire's current (post-1974) boundaries.*

Soon after Park Leaze Halt the straight route profile changed to a gentle north-easterly curve and the line entered another, longer cutting partly flanked by areas of deciduous woodland. One of these copses, about ¼ mile east of Park Leaze on the down side, was known as Railway Covert. In keeping with the gently undulating terrain through which it passed, the railway emerged from

* Coaley, closed on 4th January 1965, was re-opened as Cam & Dursley in May 1994.

Chesterton Lane Halt viewed form the overbridge, looking towards Cirencester.

Lens of Sutton

Chesterton Lane Halt and overbridge, looking towards Kemble.   *Lens of Sutton*

the long cutting to run along a short embankment which ended near a meander in the canal, which had remained south of the line since Ewen Wharf. About halfway along the embankment the branch passed over a track connecting North Furzen Leaze Farm with the Ewen-Siddington road. This bridge and Ewen Wharf are the two surviving underbridges of the route.

At the end of this embankment the line was crossed by a column of pylons. Soon after this, some 2½ miles from Kemble, the line entered two short cuttings as its route began to wind anti-clockwise towards Cirencester. Under the 1884 scheme one spur of a triangular link with the MSWJR would have diverged at this point.*

Just before the line entered a longer cutting it was crossed by Somerford Road overbridge, of which no trace remains; it had been levelled by 1973. Most of the trackbed is discernible west of this former bridge but on the east side it has been largely filled in. The cutting which extended for about ¾ mile from here through Cirencester's southern outskirts to Chesterton Lane has partly disappeared beneath a sewage depot and the Love Lane industrial estate. It was at the northern extremity of this cutting that the route came closest to the MSWJ line; hence an earlier 1883 scheme for a triangular junction here to connect the two systems.

On the west side of the line north of Love Lane the line skirted some allotments. As the branch approached Chesterton Lane overbridge it was within ½ mile of the MSWJ Watermoor station. **Chesterton Lane Halt** was sited on the up side of the line on the Cirencester side of the bridge at 94 miles 49 chains from Paddington, or just over 3½ miles from Kemble. Unlike Park Leaze Halt, it opened from the start of railbus operation yet the two halts were of almost identical design. But whereas the path leading to Park Leaze Halt created an entrance at the Cirencester end of the rear of the platform, Chesterton Lane Halt lay in a shallow cutting somewhat further from the road so that access was by means of a longer path which terminated at the Kemble end of the platform.

The route continued its north-westerly course to pass under Querns Hill about ¼ mile beyond the halt. This overbridge was demolished with the building of the town's Western Bypass, which briefly cuts across the trackbed. The former bridge was opposite a scout hut where Querns Hill divided three ways into Cotswold Avenue, Mount Street and Somerford Road. By 1977, when the road junction had been realigned, the railway cutting immediately north of Chesterton Lane had disappeared beneath Meadow Way, the feeder road to a new housing estate. The cutting is still discernible as a footpath between this estate and the new junction of Querns Hill/Somerford Road.

Cirencester station and yard

Just beyond Querns Hill bridge was the throat of the station yard. A ground frame controlled a turnout from the running line to a scissors crossover giving access to a runround (the only such facility in use during the final freight-only period) and also to a long siding, with a headshunt alongside a pig dock. The

* C. Maggs, *The Midland and South Western Junction Railway*, David & Charles, 1967.

Cirencester engine shed on 21st August, 1960.   *Roger Carpenter*

Cirencester's engine shed and water tower on 18th July, 1964. Notice the signal minus its arm.
J.M. Tolson/Corinium Museum/Cotswold District Council

Cirencester station. *Reproduced from the 25", 1921 Ordnance Survey Map*

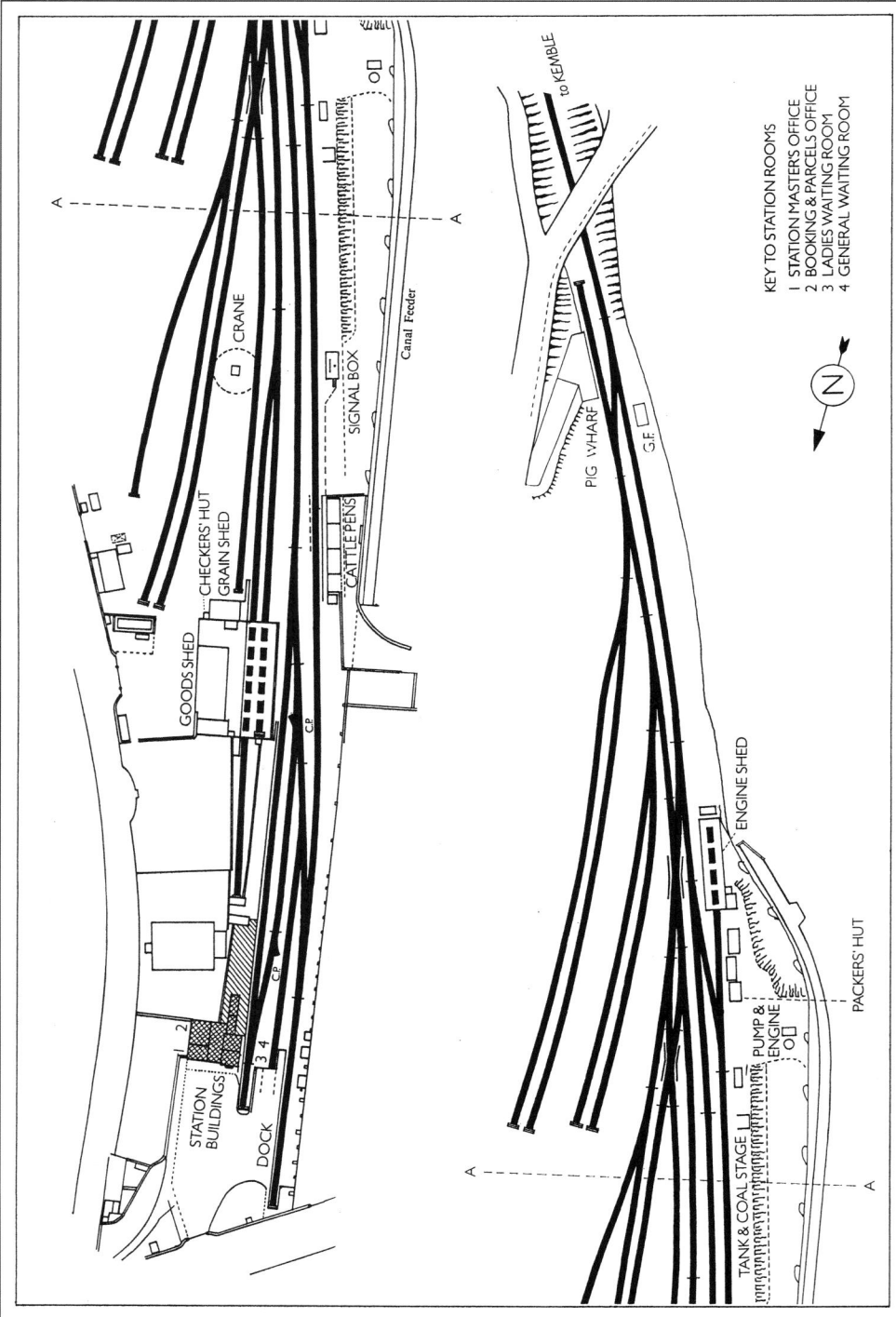

KEY TO STATION ROOMS

1 STATION MASTER'S OFFICE
2 BOOKING & PARCELS OFFICE
3 LADIES WAITING ROOM
4 GENERAL WAITING ROOM

to KEMBLE

Canal Feeder

SIGNAL BOX

CATTLE PENS

CHECKERS' HUT

GRAIN SHED

GOODS SHED

CRANE

C.P.

C.P.

STATION BUILDINGS

DOCK

1 2

3 4

PIG WHARF

G.F.

ENGINE SHED

PACKERS' HUT

PUMP & ENGINE

TANK & COAL STAGE

N

The front view of Cirencester signal box with signalman Alec Deakins at the open window c. 1940.

Frank Deakins Collection

Cirencester cattle dock and signal box, looking towards Kemble.
Railprint/Corinium Museum/Cotswold District Council

A view of Cirencester goods shed and station from the vicinity of the signal box.
Corinium Museum/Cotswold District Council

ground frame, released by a key on the line's Electric Train Staff, allowed the working of sidings which may have been difficult for the signalman to see because of the position of the engine shed. The pig dock was accessed by a path from Querns Hill and was not far from the Roman Amphitheatre, which lay to the opposite side of the running line.

The extensive goods yard stretched from the pig dock alongside Querns Hill almost to the boundary wall of the hospital, alongside the station buildings. All the freight facilities were on the up side, with entrances to the yard from Sheep Street, except for the cattle dock which was situated beside the cattle market on the down side. The cattle dock was about half way down a long siding which extended from Milepost 95 near the engine shed to another loading dock just beyond the station buffer stops. The engine shed was accessed by a trailing connection from this siding, which was also bordered by the coaling stage, water tower and signal box as well as by various small huts. A feeder of the Thames & Severn Canal ran just to the west of this siding from the cattle pens past the engine shed, supplying the water tower. The latter structure was unusual in housing a water column within the tall slim stone base of the tower.

The original broad gauge engine shed was replaced in 1872 by a gable roofed wooden building which remained in use until the passenger service closure. It had a brick lean-to office with chimney, on the canal side of the front entrance. The shed siding was provided with a wheelstop to discourage engines from running away, as the station complex sloped towards the town centre. The key to the padlocked wheelstop was kept in the signal box.*

The signal box, a gable-roofed structure on the canal side of the long siding, was not far from the cattle pens and virtually opposite the goods yard crane. The spacious goods yard on the east side of the layout included a substantial goods shed, originally wooden but rebuilt in metal with extended platforms in 1938. One track emerged from the goods shed as far as the Kemble end of the station platform. John Nicholas recalls that the goods shed was still standing in 1973, but it disappeared when the yard and station throat were redeveloped for light industry and a new road a few years later.

The main station building, which survives today, was designed by Brunel and its construction supervised by Charles Richardson. A three-storey structure in two sections, each with a steep gable roof, it has been described as an example of Gothic revival 'piled high with fanciful turrets, pinnacles and ornamentations'. These were the words of J.M. Rogers in a prize essay which also claimed that station architecture became more subdued, except at the largest stations, after the Railway Mania of 1844-5 because railways no longer had to assert themselves.† He argued that had the line opened say 10 years later, its terminus might well have been of more modest design but it was more probably the scarcity of capital for railway projects in the early 1850s which cut mid-Victorian stations down to size.

The original station buildings included an overall roof which extended to the western boundary wall but was removed in 1874; the platform canopy may well date from this period.

The 1956 alterations were mainly to the single storey portion of the building, which included the station master's and parcels' offices. On the forecourt side

* R.H. Clark, *An Historical Survey of Selected Great Western Stations*, Volume 2, OPC, 1979.
† J.M. Rogers, essay reproduced in *Gloucestershire Countryside*, December 1963.

Cirencester station viewed from the Kemble end of the platform, prior to 1956 rebuilding.
Lens of Sutton

The rebuilt station at Cirencester viewed from a similar position.   *Lens of Sutton*

The parcel office entrance viewed from the platform, prior to 1956 rebuilding.
Railprint/Corinium Museum/Cotswold District Council

Cirencester station building viewed from the buffer stop prior to 1956 rebuilding.
Lens of Sutton

Cirencester station from the buffer stops prior to rebuilding, with an 0-6-0PT running round its train.   *Lens of Sutton*

A view of the rebuilt station at Cirencester with a railbus at the platform. In the distance the signal box and engine shed can be seen.   *Lens of Sutton*

it gained a bland steel and glass canopy, lacking sympathy with the building as a whole and more in keeping with the long fanlight windows added to the parcel office frontage and on the platform side walls of the lavatories. Similar windows, running immediately below the ceiling, featured in the 1970 rebuilding of Oxford station and also at Purton, rebuilt a few years before its closure to passengers from 2nd November, 1964 but still standing.

The traditional platform canopy was retained and survived, along with the single storey platform building, until about 1974. But features which were removed in 1956 included a ground floor bay window at the front of the main building as well as an attractive glass skylight roof over the entrance lobby. Despite these architectural losses, the station is without doubt the most impressive survivor of the line's history.

The building has defied attempts to redevelop the former passenger station. David Viner believes that plans existed at the time of closure to build a shoe factory on the site. In 1973 planning permission was given to convert the old building to a bus station, resulting in removal of the platform canopy. In 1977 Cotswold District Council, which had superseded Cirencester UDC as planning authority, applied to demolish the station because it stood in the way of a proposed multi-storey car park. Vigorous objections at the resulting public inquiry included those from Cirencester Town Council, the Council for British Architecture and Gloucestershire Society for Industrial Archaeology, the latter represented by Revd W. Awdry. The Secretary of State for the Environment rejected the scheme in 1978.

District Councillors responded positively to this decision, authorising extensive repairs to the interior of the building which were made in 1980. By this time the forecourt was no longer used as a bus station and the bus service to Kemble had been drastically reduced.

A printing firm rented the premises for a few years but then ceased trading and the building became empty. Another proposal for demolition in favour of a car park was made in 1988 but councillors were persuaded to abandon the plans on the strength of convincing evidence of Brunel's personal influence on the design. The Council's Director of Planning was quoted later in the year as saying that developers he had spoken with saw the old station as an asset rather than a disadvantage to any scheme.*

Property speculation may well have helped rob the town of its trains, so it is perhaps ironic that the slump in this form of trading in more recent years should have prevented the bulldozers from erasing all trace of Cirencester's railway heritage. Nevertheless, a new Waitrose store was opened on the site of the goods yard and station throat in November 1995. If the branch were to be revived in the next century, a new terminus would be needed in the Somerford Road area.

---

* *Gloucestershire Echo*, 10.11.88.

Appendix One

The Railway Career of Daniel Bingham

One of Cirencester's most famous sons and benefactors spent his formative years as a clerk at the Town station. Born in 1830, Daniel George Bingham was the third youngest of four sons of a local trunk maker, also called Daniel, who lived in Black Jack Street. His extensive obituary in the *Wilts & Gloucestershire Standard* in March 1913 recorded that he joined the C&GWUR 'not many years after the opening of the line to Cirencester but before it was extended (from Kemble) to Gloucester'. This suggests 1844 as the most likely date for his entry into the service as it seems doubtful that he could have begun railway employment before his 14th birthday. The C&GWUR had of course been absorbed by the Great Western in 1843 but the old name no doubt remained in local currency; commercial directories continued to refer to the line by its original name in their descriptions of Cirencester.

Bingham's career had its origin in his lifelong friendship with James Staats Forbes, appointed district manager at Cirencester station during the transition to Great Western ownership. Forbes took up lodgings with the Binghams and took a great liking to young Daniel, for whom he secured a junior clerical position at the station. Within a few years the GWR had promoted Forbes, first to divisional superintendent at Cheltenham and then to chief goods manager, Paddington. Bingham subsequently gained promotion to his patron's office in London.

Forbes' high reputation as a railway manager and his connections with the Netherlands resulted in his being appointed in 1851 to head the Dutch - Rhenish Railways, then on the verge of bankruptcy. Given a free hand to implement any changes he considered were necessary, he soon assembled 'a group of chief officers of exceptional ability' (*Wilts & Gloucestershire Standard*, 8.3.1913). Daniel Bingham was invited to join this dynamic team in 1858 and took up the position of chief goods manager. He made his mark by securing trainloads of coal from Westphalia to Holland, returning with Spanish ores from Rotterdam.

Bingham effected such a transformation of the railway freight business in Holland that, on Forbes' return to England in 1861 to manage the London, Chatham & Dover Railway, he was appointed to succeed his master. Daniel was then only 31 and had married Jane Brain, of Kelmscott near Fairford, the previous year.

Soon after taking command, Bingham discovered that most of the company's staff were woefully underpaid while higher officials drew what he considered to be excessive salaries. Realising that motivation of the mainstream workforce was crucial for a successful business, he improved pay substantially for the bulk of the employees. Dismissing the inevitable protests from vested interests, he retorted, 'I am going to make these men work and to do this I must see that they are paid'.

Remaining in charge until the Dutch - Rhenish Railway was nationalised in 1890, Bingham had produced such a turnround of the company's finances that the Netherlands Government paid 25 per cent over and above the value of each share, although these had been considered worthless 40 years earlier.

Bingham's generosity did not stop at his employees. When nationalisation brought about his retirement from railway service, he was handsomely compensated and set about the improvement of amenities in Cirencester, which he regularly visited despite keeping his permanent home in Utrecht. He endowed the construction and staffing of a new public library and also the building of the Bingham Hall, intended for educational lectures, in 1908.

Daniel died in Utrecht in March 1913. He and Jane had no children but a glowing tribute in the *Wilts & Gloucestershire Standard* commented that no worthy cause had ever appealed to his open heart and purse in vain.

Appendix Two

Signalling on the Branch

When opened in 1841, the line from Swindon to Cirencester was worked on the time interval system and protected by disc and crossbar signals, operated by policemen. By 1870, the now branch line from Cirencester to Kemble was worked by Train Staff, the normal system employed by the GWR on short, single track routes which had only one block section.

The 1890 Service Timetable shows the branch as worked by Train Staff and Ticket, the ticket being of the round type and red in colour. Interestingly, the same document listed the Tetbury branch, opened only the previous year, as being worked by Train Staff and Disc Block Telegraph. The Board of Trade had wanted Block Telegraph used together with Train Staff and Ticket as an additional safety device; the precise date of its installation on the Cirencester branch is unclear, but it is shown as the system of working the line in the 1896 service timetable.

Signal Boxes

The final Cirencester Town signal box was opened in 1892 and was a 19-lever Double Twist frame. This type had levers at 5¼ inches apart, centre to centre, and was widely used because it saved companies having to pay hefty fees to the Stevens company which patented the superior tappet frame, which later became standard when Stevens forgot to renew the patent. The box outlasted the branch passenger service by only two months, closing on 14th June, 1964, when much of the trackwork at the terminus was taken out of use and the branch was downgraded to one-train working until its final closure to all traffic.

The box which opened at Kemble in 1929 was a vertical tappet three-bar frame with 69 levers, increased to 70 in 1941. It replaced two earlier boxes at either end of the station and was itself closed on 29th June, 1968 when colour light signals controlled from Swindon Panel box replaced semaphores on that stretch of the Gloucester main line.

Kemble East box, sited beside the down main line opposite the junction, was in use by 1884 and controlled in its early years the Train Staff and Ticket system used on the branch, until that system was superseded by the Webb-Thompson large Electric Train Staff (ETS) in the 1890s.*

The line was converted to Electric Token working on Sunday 12th August, 1945. Cirencester Town box opened specially at 7 am when a staff was withdrawn at Kemble enabling the engineers' motor trolley to occupy the branch. The staff was kept out until completion of the work, scheduled to finish at 5 pm, over an hour before the first train. The district signalling inspector was required to make arrangements for protection of the line, including appointment of handsignalmen.

The work involved replacement of ETS apparatus by new Token Instruments at both ends of the route. A new combined ringing key and bell with a Token Control Instrument was installed in Kemble signal box. The ETS Instrument was removed also from the cabin on the bay platform at Kemble and its place taken by an Electric Token Instrument with 10 tokens and five token carriers. A similar machine now superseded the ETS equipment in Cirencester Town box, while the ground frame opposite the pig dock was provided with a Token Release Lock after disconnection of the Annett's Key Release Lock.

* Research undertaken by L. Crosier, Signalling Record Society, 1994.

The Branch Ground Frame at Kemble

The Sectional Appendix to the 1914 Service Timetable refers to a ground frame, wire-locked from Kemble East box, and housing the Electric Train Staff instrument for the branch. Larry Crosier believes this ground frame to have been commissioned at the same time as the first Kemble box. The 1914 instructions required the shunter to deliver the Kemble-Cirencester ETS between Kemble East box and the driver of the Cirencester branch train; by contrast it was the porter who was responsible for taking the Tetbury branch ETS between Kemble West box and the Tetbury driver.

As described in Chapter Ten, the ground frame was moved to the bay platform when the new signal box opened in 1929. This provided an extra safeguard against the wrong ETS being handed over, but another reason for the relocation of the ground frame was that the new box was further away from some of the points at the Cirencester end of the bay platform sidings than the East box had been; the maximum permitted distance for manual operation of points from a signal box or ground frame was 350 yards.

Occupation Key System

Larry Crosier advises that this had been installed by 1914, well before most Great Western branches which had to await the Government Loans Scheme of the 1930s before they were equipped with it.* The system worked equally well with either the Electric Train Staff or Electric Token systems. It enabled Permanent Way Gangs to occupy part of the route without any risk of a train entering the stretch of line under possession.

Such an arrangement was achieved by means of the Ganger's Occupation Key, which controlled an instrument provided at one of six locations along the branch, i.e. Kemble bay platform (where the Train Staff Instrument, operated by a porter or shunter, had been superseded by the Token Instrument in 1945); Cirencester Town signal box and four intermediate telephone huts.

When the ganger held the Occupation Key, he had absolute possession of the branch and did not need to protect the line with handsignalmen or detonators. The system represented a businesslike investment by railway companies to reduce their infrastructure costs at a time when their passenger traffic had been hit by the economic slump and growing road competition.

Occupation of the line might be required to change a rail, repair the permanent way or merely to move the ganger's inspection trolley from one part of the branch to another. The normal procedure, if an occupation was required for a short period between trains, was for the ganger to advise the Cirencester Town signalman, who then turned the commutator of his Key Control Instrument from No. 1 (Normal) to No. 2 position. The Kemble signalman had to press in the bell key of his Token Control Instrument; doing so unlocked the commutator of the Key Control Instrument at Cirencester Town which had then to be turned to the No. 4 position. The ganger was then able to withdraw the key from the Key Token Instrument in the telephone hut nearest him. This resulted in both signal boxes' Token Instruments being locked so that no token could be withdrawn for the passage of a train.

Giving up the occupation involved similar co-operation between the ganger and the two signal boxes. He was expected to surrender possession of the line at the agreed time but could return the occupation key to any of the Instruments applicable to his gang and controlled by the same pair of signal boxes. When he replaced the key, he had to turn it until the indicator showed No. 1 position and then telephone Cirencester Town signal box.

* PRO Ref. RAIL 1136/32.

But the Cirencester signalman was not required when the ganger's possessions took place when the branch was normally closed, i.e. on Sunday mornings or in the small hours.   A notice in the GWR's weekly engineering book would stipulate that the Occupation Key had to be drawn after the last train had cleared the section on the Saturday. When a Sunday or night occupation of the branch was completed, the ganger would return the Occupation Key to a small padlocked box fixed near the door of Town signal box for the signalman to collect and reinstate in his Key Release Instrument when he next came on duty.

In 1960, Cirencester Town Permanent Way gang covered the branch between the terminus and a point about ¼ mile from Kemble. A Velocipede Inspection Car and a mechanical trolley were then used on the branch.

Whistle and bell codes

The 1896 Service Timetable listed engine whistle codes to be used at Cirencester as follows:

For movements to/from Kemble, one whistle; from platform line to run-round train, two whistles; to/from goods shed, three whistles; to/from mileage yard, one whistle, one crow; to/from water tank line, four short whistles.

A branch train approaching Kemble had to sound two long whistles at signals. When the locomotive ran round its train there, one whistle was required.

In 1960, branch trains approaching Kemble were required to sound two short and one long whistle at signals, because of the difficulty the signalman had in seeing the branch from his box, near the down main platform. Similarly, a branch train or locomotive needing to foul the main line had to give one crow and two short whistles on reaching signals. Railbuses would sound their hooters in such circumstances.

Bells made communication between the signalman and fireman easier at Cirencester, where the box was a considerable distance from the platform buffer stops. Push buttons and cards listing the ringing codes were provided in the signal box and on the platform stop block.

Signalman Alec Deakins pulling levers in Kemble signal box.   *Frank Deakins Collection*

Appendix Three

Arrangements for the Royal Train, 22nd May, 1946

All the following details have been gleaned from GWR Notice of Royal Trains No. 40, produced on 18th May, 1946 (*see also Chapter Six*).

Train preparation

The empty Royal Train was to be stabled on No. 18 Shed Road at Old Oak Common depot and was due off Old Oak Common East Signal Box at 8.55 on the morning of departure. The ECS train was to be worked into Platform 1 at Paddington. The train engine, No. 5056 *Earl of Powis* was due to pass Old Oak Common East at 9.10, exactly an hour before it was scheduled to take out the loaded train.

The formation of the train (from the engine) leaving Paddington, described in the circular as 'all GW stock' with a total weight of 219½ tons and length of 385 feet 9 inches (both excluding engine), was as follows:

7370	Brake Compo (Brake end leading),
9006	Saloon (Kitchen end leading),
9001	Saloon (Kitchen end trailing),
9002	Saloon (Kitchen end trailing),
7290	Compo (first class compartments leading),
6550	Brake Compo (Brake end trailing).

The station master, Paddington, was required to advise his opposite number at Cirencester Town (Mr C. Feldwick) and the divisional operating superintendent, Gloucester (Mr R.H.B. Nicholls) when the train had left Paddington.

Alterations to main line working

The train was booked to run on the down main line throughout from Paddington to Kemble, using the down through line at Swindon station. A few small break-section signal boxes, such as Circourt (between Wantage Road and Challow) and Coates (at the site of Tetbury Road station) were to be specially opened to increase line capacity.

To avoid delaying the special, due through Swindon at 11.57 am, the 11.20 am Swindon-Cheltenham was required to depart punctually and the 11.55 am, Swindon-Kemble local was to be held in the station until the Royal Train had cleared Loco Yard box.

Alterations to the branch service

Two passenger trains each way were cancelled, i.e. 11.15 am ex-Cirencester, 11.55 am ex-Kemble, 12.25 pm ex-Cirencester and 1.05 pm ex-Kemble. This was to keep the branch clear not only for the Royal Train itself but also for the associated shunting movements at Kemble and the Light Engine and ECS workings along the branch.

Instructions to Signalmen

The Kemble signalman had to send the 'Blocking Back outside Home Signal' code to Coates (to block the up line) 15 minutes before the Royal Train was due at Kemble. After receiving a 'Line Clear' bell signal from Coates (for the down line), he was able to return 'Line Clear' to Minety, the box in his rear (two block sections always had to be clear for a Royal Train). Immediately after doing so, Kemble had to obtain 'Line Clear' from Cirencester Town.

The Electric Token for the branch had to be withdrawn by the Kemble station foreman and handed to the driver of locomotive No. 5506, which was waiting on the bay platform line.

Coates box, due to open at 11.05 that morning, was required to remain open for the duration of the shunting of the Royal Train at Kemble and until after the train had left Kemble and an 'Obstruction Removed' signal had been received from Kemble to reopen the up line.

Shunting of the Royal Train at Kemble

There was no facing crossover from the down main line to the branch at the Swindon end of Kemble station at this time and in any case a 'Castle' class locomotive was not permitted over the branch. A complicated manoeuvre was planned using two '45XX' class 2-6-2Ts to cross the train from the down to the up platform line and then over the junction.

1. No. 5506 (with chimney facing Gloucester) and No. 5534 (facing Swindon) were to be placed on the Cirencester bay line 30 minutes before the Royal Train was due.
2. 15 minutes before the special was due, handsignalmen had to be in position at points Nos. 16 (down main to down siding); 47 (branch to loop) and 52 (up main crossover). These points were to be clipped and padlocked in the normal position.
3. Once Coates box had acknowledged the 'Blocking Back outside Home Signal' message, No. 5534 was to set back from the branch bay to the up main line and to come to a stand in front of Crossover Points No. 21.
4. The Royal Train, headed by No. 5056, would run to a point beyond the crossover at the Gloucester end of the station, stopping with the centre of the footplate opposite a white post on the driver's side on the up side of the up main line.
5. After a handsignal had confirmed that the train was at a stand clear of crossover points No. 21, these were to be set, clipped and padlocked so that No. 5534 could cross over to the down main line and be coupled by its fireman to the rear of the Royal Train.
6. Once No. 5534 had been coupled, No. 5056 would be detached by its fireman and remain stationary until the Royal Train had left Kemble.
7. Crossover points No. 21 had to remain clipped and padlocked for the train to proceed on to the up main line, where it would be brought to a stand with the centre of No. 5534's footplate opposite a black and white post on the driver's side on the down side of the down main line.
8. Once the train had halted clear of points No. 48, the handsignalman there had to give a hand signal to the Kemble signalman, who would then set these points for the branch line.
9. No. 5506 would then set back from the branch bay platform to the up main line and be attached to the train by its fireman. The fireman of No. 5534 then had to uncouple his own locomotive. The Royal Train was now allowed to leave Kemble. No. 5534 had to remain on the up main until the special was well clear of Kemble but would then proceed to the branch platform loop.

Arrangements at Cirencester

Passengers were excluded from Town station platform and approach road, which also had to be cleared of all vehicles except Royal cars, from 12.10 pm until the Royal party had left the station.

The signalman at Cirencester Town was not to send 'Train out of Section' to Kemble until the Royal party had left the station platform.

Empty stock and light engine movements over the branch

The empty train was scheduled to leave Cirencester at 1.05 pm, 'carrying "A" class headlamps and to be signalled accordingly', read the Notice. The ECS was to be given priority over any conflicting trains, such as the 1.10 pm Kemble-Swindon stopper which had to be held back until the empty stock had cleared Kemble.

The two tank locomotives divided the honours of hauling the Royal carriages as follows:

No. 5534 to run light from Kemble at 12.50, due Cirencester at 12.58 to work the 1.05 pm ECS to Swindon, due to pass Kemble at 1.15 and to arrive Swindon at 1.37 pm.

No. 5506 to run light from Cirencester at 1.27 pm, direct to Swindon, whence it would work the same carriages to Badminton.

(No. 5056 was booked to run light from Kemble at 12.35 pm for servicing at Swindon shed, then light to Badminton via the Westerleigh triangle where it would reverse.)

Contingencies

Nothing was left to chance. Breakdown Gangs and cranes were to be in readiness at Old Oak Common, Reading and Swindon for both legs of the journey. Standby engines were required at these same depots for the outward journey (and also at Bristol for the return journey). All staff issued with a copy of the special notice had to immediately confirm receipt by telegram to their Divisional Superintendent.

Any tunnel to be traversed by a Royal Train had to be inspected and protected under the terms of Clause 16 of the company's standard instructions for Royal Trains. Kemble tunnel, just short of the branch junction, was the only tunnel involved in the outward journey, and had to be inspected by competent Permanent Way staff shortly before the special was due through it. No other train was then allowed to enter the tunnel until after the Royal Train had passed through.

Additional precautions included the stationing of a handsignalman at each end of the tunnel to prevent unauthorised access at least an hour before the train was due. If possible, a man was to be positioned on top of the tunnel beside each ventilation shaft, also an hour before the Royal special was due.

Appendix Four

Traffic Statistics for Cirencester Town, 1903-1959

The two complementary sources were the GWR *Traffic Records for the Gloucester Division*, 1925-59 (Public Record Office ref. RAIL 266) and the bound GWR volume *Traffic dealt with at certain stations* (Clinker Collection, Brunel University). The statistics in the PRO are handwritten, whereas the bound volume of divisional booklets in the Clinker Collection are printed records. This may account for small discrepancies arising from different definitions of a particular type of traffic, or retrospective adjustments to reflect refunds, audit etc.

(Key: P= Passenger & Sundries (including car parking and toilets); Pcls= Parcels & Miscellaneous; L= Livestock; Frt= Freight; 'Other' includes rents and tolls.)

Revenue (£)

Year	Staff		P	Pcls	L	Frt	Other	Total
	Nos.	Costs						
1903	16	1,068	8,335	4,072		15,929		28,336
1913	18	1,337	8,404	4,147		20,210		32,761
1923	24	3,903	10,201	7,039		29,524		46,764
1925	29	4,206	10,113	5,306	2,981	28,549	353	47,302
1926	29	3,939	8,501	5,204	3,172	29,327	266	46,470
1927	29	4,090	8,809	5,087	4,818	30,624	288	49,626
1928	29	4,024	8,219	5,504	3,779	28,241	469	46,212
1929	28	3,828	7,263	5,938	3,154	25,979	428	42,762
1930	28	3,896	6,495	5,397	2,526	24,878	553	39,849
1931	27	3,792	5,606	4,842	4,395	23,332	636	38,811
1932	26	3,944	5,036	4,431	3,388	21,729	491	35,075
1933	24	3,928	4,702	3,750	1,948	23,359	577	34,336
1934	24	3,977	4,725	3,697	4,338	26,825	764	40,349
1935	27	4,242	4,858	2,160	8,011	24,747		39,776
1936	26	4,287	5,120	2,119	8,186	27,843		43,268
1937	27	4,366	6,522	2,013	1,932	30,130		40,597
1938	27	4,460	7,103	2,066	2,052	29,958		41,179
1939	27	4,462	8,539	2,106	1,596	28,704		40,945
1940	27	5,910	10,760	Not completed in PRO records				
1941	29	6,668	14,006	2,358				
1942	29	7,266	18,275	2,252				
1943	29	9,692	28,007	3,003				
1944	29	10,898	24,400	2,974				

The PRO records show no figures for Freight receipts or total station revenue after 1939, nor of Paybill costs after 1949. The latter year was when British Railways set up the

Branch Line Committee, whose purpose was to select lines for possible closure. As a reaction to this, there may have been a policy decision in the Gloucester traffic district not to record staff costs by station because these could give a misleading impression of unprofitability, particularly now that freight receipts were being included within the totals for larger stations, e.g. Cirencester Town's freight traffic was included in the total for Swindon.

Revenue (£)

Year	Staff Nos.	Costs	Passenger & Sundries *	Parcels & Misc.
1945	29	10,793	23,637	3,129
1946	29	11,889	21,869	2,471
1947	29	13,240	19,888	3,412
1948	29	14,325	14,515	5,930
1949	29	13,928	14,328	4,262
1950			11,863	3,762
1951			12,054	3,700
1952	36		12,500	4,504
1953	36		12,631	4,321
1954	36		11,607	4,863
1955	36		10,208	5,066
1956	36		10,552	6,568
1957	36		11,869	6,903
1958	30		10,476	8,414
1959	30		12,583	7,152

* includes cab rents, car parking and toilet receipts.

The PRO does not appear to have any traffic statistics for 1960 onwards. It is tempting to agree with David Henshaw (op. cit) that such results were suppressed or destroyed because they provided evidence against the closure programme.

Tickets issued; Parcels forwarded and received, Cirencester Town, 1903-59

Year	Tickets issued Journey	Seasons	Parcels Forwarded	Parcels Received
1903	47,211	*	*	*
1913	45,516	*	*	*
1923	37,376	88	*	*
1925	36,546	122	16,829	29,347
1926	30,310	85	15,172	29,857
1927	30,652	89	17,692	31,873
1928	28,453	96	17,781	36,179
1929	25,860	85	16,690	38,790

* Season Tickets were not recorded for these dates in printed GWR records, which show *total* number of Parcels handled at the station as follows: 1903, 46,736; 1913, 60,722; 1923, 49,673.

Year	Tickets issued Journey	Seasons	Parcels Forwarded	Parcels Received
1930	22,009	64	16,084	40,776
1931	19,767	52	14,951	41,462
1932	18,202	34	15,012	44,250
1933	16,821	26	13,812	49,174
1934	16,523	25	13,663	50,881
1935	17,821	23	12,998	53,578
1936	20,231	34	12,140	57,275
1937	24,284	51	11,921	59,700
1938	25,460	32	12,274	61,337
1939	24,720	31	12,738	60,950
1940	25,473	42	13,960	53,965
1941	33,735	90	14,240	47,453
1942	48,575	60	14,122	42,671
1943	56,353	93	15,730	45,017
1944	52,769	98	18,148	49,893
1945	48,460	93	16,877	43,901
1946	38,207	136	14,265	43,335
1947	32,438	81	15,327	48,486
1948	22,795	39	19,077	51,419
1949	23,329	137	18,201	49,994
1950	21,374	153	16,454	51,896
1951	21,570	137	17,006	54,238
1952	22,197	118	15,611	58,191
1953	23,338	105	14,633	56,295
1954	22,278	170	15,724	49,602
1955	19,790	120	18,338	50,326
1956	19,549	150	21,978	47,119
1957	21,982	130	21,641	53,211
1958	19,262	194	24,433	56,101
1959	30,427	215	19,202	60,007

Sources: GWR *Traffic dealt with at certain stations* (Clinker Collection) for 1903-23; PR0 ref. RAIL 266 from 1925 onwards.

The number of season tickets issued at Cirencester Town was very low when compared with small main line stations in Gloucestershire such as Chalford and Churchdown, which enjoyed more intensive, direct services to larger centres of population. By contrast, the only feasible destinations for commuting from Cirencester Town were Stroud and Swindon, largely because the earliest train from Town station was at around 8 am.

Note also the large increase in tickets issued in 1959, the first year of railbus operation. But the increase in revenue was slight (see the Revenue Table earlier in this Appendix), which tends to confirm my belief that the railbuses attracted local rather than longer distance passengers.

Milk cans forwarded from Cirencester Town, 1925-1946
(Source: PRO ref. RAIL 266.)

Year	Total cans	£	Year	Total cans	£
1925	12,780	991	1935	251	15
1926	11,115	882	1936	1,488	93
1927	13,412	1,014	1937	552	33
1928	14,746	956	1938	79	6
1929	15,862	956	1939	340	26
1930	16,530	988	1940	47	4
1931	8,809	523			
1932	6,683	413	1941-6	0	0
1933	87	5			
1934	0	0	1947-51	Not recorded	

Milk forwarded from Cirencester Town, 1952-1959

	Gallons	Cases	£
1952	858	286	21
1953	1,023	341	24
1954	1,371	457	36
1955	657	219	19
1956	1,101	367	29
1957	1,041	356	27
1958		180	20
1959		156	not recorded

Livestock wagons forwarded from Cirencester Town, 1903-50
Sources: GWR *Traffic dealt with at certain stations* for 1903-23; PRO ref. RAIL 266 from 1925.

Year	Total wagons	£	Year	Total wagons	£
1903	858		1935	2,267	8,011
			1936	2,485	8,186
1913	825		1937	677	1,932
			1938	623	2,052
1923	965		1939	608	1,596
1925	1,027	2,981	1940	804	not recorded
1926	1,050	3,172	1941	550	
1927	1,253	4,818	1942	372	
1928	1,099	3,779	1943	309	
1929	1,027	3,154	1944	137	
1930	836	2,526	1945	202	
1931	925	4,395	1946	144	
1932	734	3,388	1947	114	
1933	580	1,948	1948	71	
1934	1,356	4,338	1949	83	
			1950	66	

Appendix Five

Arrangements for Operating the Branch After its Closure to Passengers

The following has been gleaned from a BR internal memo, undated but evidently composed shortly after the Ministerial decision on the passenger service:

British Railways (Western Region)

Withdrawal of Passenger Train Services - Cirencester and Tetbury branches.

The Minister of Transport has approved the withdrawal of the light weight diesel rail buses from the above mentioned branches as from Monday 6th April, 1964. Details of the staff affected by the proposals together with vacancies which are available for staff who will become redundant are set out in the attached.

Until such time as freight facilities are withdrawn from Cirencester Town and the branch completely closed, the following arrangements will apply:

Supervision
To be supervised by the Kemble station master.

Signalling Arrangements
To be worked as a siding from Kemble. If the necessary signal alterations have not been completed by Monday 6th April a signalman to be retained at Cirencester Town until the alterations are finished.

Parcels Arrangements
Collected & Delivered and 'Station to Station' parcels to continue to be dealt with as now.

The existing arrangements for the loading of a van at Kemble overnight with parcels traffic and the conveyance of the van attached to the early morning freight to continue. The freight must be held at Kemble until the arrival of the 6.35 am Swindon passenger service for the transference of fish traffic to the van. The new departure time of the freight will be 7.15 am.

A further van will be provided at Kemble to trip parcels to Cirencester with the engine of the 7.15 am freight as follows:

			am	am
Cirencester	(Light Engine)	dep.		10.30
Kemble		arr.	10.40	10.50
Cirencester		arr.	11.00	

The two vans to return to Kemble (with any outward parcels available at that time) by the return freight service retimed to leave Cirencester at 11.30 am. Other outward parcels to be taken into Kemble by the Cirencester parcels car.

Payment of wages
To be dealt with by the Kemble station master utilising the proposed new bus service.

Revenue cash

To be conveyed to Kemble in a locked cash bag by the Cirencester parcels vehicle and remitted from that point as at present.

The same document tabulated the current staffing position on both branches and the effect in the short term of the passenger closure and in the longer term of plans to convey Cirencester's freight by road from Swindon.

Cirencester Town then had an establishment of 18 posts of which three were vacant. Closing the passenger service would remove nine of these posts, namely the station master, one clerk, a goods porter, a station porter, two signalmen, two railbus drivers and a passenger guard. (All four staff based at Tetbury, comprising a railbus driver, two passenger guards and a senior porter, were also facing imminent redundancy.)

Vacancies available to redundant staff were listed, including signalmen's posts at Badminton, Chipping Sodbury, Minety and Purton, all in the same grade (Class 4) as those redundant at Cirencester Town. Clerical and shunting posts were on offer at Swindon, as were positions as porter at Stroud and leading porter at Charfield and Hullavington. The railway was then still a very labour intensive industry, although many of these alternative jobs were themselves to disappear within a few years as more stations and mechanical signal boxes closed.

The nine staff who would remain to deal with freight and parcels traffic at Cirencester were to lose their jobs under the Swindon freight concentration proposals, as were three porters and three shunters at Kemble.

Bibliography

Kemble, Ewen and Poole Keynes, C. Brann, Collectors' Books, 1992.

'The Poor Dear Great Western', J. Thomas (Chapter in C. Brann book above.)

'Railbuses Extant', B. Hancock and M. Brown, *Railway Magazine*, August 1979.

GWR Country Stations: 2, C.J. Leigh, Ian Allan, 1984.

GWR Junction Stations, A. Vaughan, Ian Allan, 1988.

'The Branch Lines from Kemble', C.G. Maggs, *Railway World*, December 1958.

The British Railcar, R.M. Tufnell, David & Charles, 1984.

Cirencester Town station: an outline history, D. Viner. Report to Cirencester development subcommittee, Cotswold District Council, 1988.

Cirencester: a History and Guide, J. Welsford, Alan Sutton, 1987.

Official Handbook of Stations, British Transport Commission, 1956.

Railway Magazine, April 1958.

Brunel University Transport Collection prints are available from W.R. Burton, 3 Fairway, Clifton, York, YO3 6QA.